The Nonbeliever's Guide
to Bible Stories

T0096017

The Nonbeliever's Guide to Bible Stories

C. B. Brooks, M.D.

PITCHSTONE PUBLISHING
Durham, North Carolina

Pitchstone Publishing
Durham, North Carolina 27705

To contact the publisher, please email info@pitchstonepublishing.com

10 9 8 7 6 5 4 3 2 1

Library of Congress Cataloging-in-Publication Data

Brooks, C. B.
 The nonbeliever's guide to Bible stories / C.B. Brooks, M.D.
   pages cm
 ISBN 978-1-63431-060-4 (pbk. : alk. paper)
 1. Bible—Criticism, interpretation, etc. 2. Bible stories, English. I. Title.
 BS511.3.B755 2015
 220.6—dc23
                2015015161

Cover image of "Jesus Calms a Storm on the Sea," used under license from
Shutterstock.com

Contents

Introduction

Congratulations—you've seen the light!

As a nonbeliever, you've overcome a major hurdle of life by avoiding or throwing off the shackles of organized religion. Whew! What a relief. No fables, fear, coercion, obligation, lunacy, jihad, guilt trips, adherence to ancient rules, birth control interference, discrimination against other groups, pressure for donations—plus you've got your weekends free!

For those who were indoctrinated into religion as a child and rejected the group delusions on your own—be proud of your maturity and independent thinking. This is a milestone of life.

For those of you who had enlightened parents who didn't force religious training and adherence on you—Alleluia. You have truly been spared an ordeal. Give those parents a big hug. You are the real "Chosen Ones."

I wrote my first book for my daughter, as a guide to successful living. *Trust Your Radar: Honest Advice for Teens and Young Adults from a Surgeon, Firefighter, Police Officer, Scuba Divemaster, Golfer, and Amateur Comedian* combined life lessons with fun stories from my varied careers. My second book, *Trust Your Radar, Slackers' Edition*, was for her friends who couldn't handle a full book. Both works identified organized religions as "jammers" of our clear-thinking "brain radars." This was, of course, controversial since religions are given a great deal of respect in many circles. They do nonetheless cause a lot of stress, problems, and misery for many people. They're also responsible for holding back scientific advancement and progress of societies as a whole.

The good news is that nonbelievers or "unaffiliated" people make up a growing percentage of younger generations throughout the world. And all indications are that this encouraging trend will continue. Everybody shout, "Amen, brother C. B.!" As a consequence, many nonbelievers—perhaps yourself included—may not have any idea what others are talking about when they reference religious stories in conversation, art, or literature.

This became apparent to me one day with my growing daughter, who was lucky enough to have escaped childhood religious programming. I remember walking into her messy room while she was surrounded by pets and stuffed animals, and saying something like, "Jesus, it looks like Noah's freaking ark in here." This volatile comment was met with a blank stare.

That got me thinking.

Our expanding demographic segment of fortunate "unaffiliated" young people probably should have some concept of the religious fairy tales being foisted upon their believing peers. At least just so they can get all the jokes. From this encounter sprang the idea for this book. Just as Cain and Able sprang from the supple loins of Eve. (Say what?! Don't worry, we'll get to it.)

This will be a mildly irreverent, whirlwind tour of the granddaddy of them all, the Holy Bible, written by God himself. Once you've heard at least a synopsis of these stories, you'll get 98 percent of the references people make. And since the Torah and Koran and the Book of Mormon all borrow from each other—you'll get enough of them too.

This book will save you a boatload of aggravation. The actual Bible is hard to read. It's tedious, often contradictory, historically imprecise, and filled with extraneous details that add nothing to the stories. There are large passages about cattle, goats, asses, other tribes, extra characters that go nowhere, concubines, harlots (prostitutes), slaves, and kooky rules. It makes me suspect that believers really haven't read it all and just parrot the highlights. We'll hit those highlights to give you the gist of it and further your knowledge base. And don't worry, I'm certainly not pushing a religious agenda. I'm a fervent nonbeliever!

Hearken unto me my children, here is our mission: To have fun and fill your memory banks with cherry-picked stories—simply so you'll know what they're babbling about.

Together, we'll take it head-on, chapter by chapter.

Author's note: Throughout the Bible, God is referred to with the male pronoun, he. But since he's God, the H is capitalized, so he is He or Him. It's one of the perks of being the Almighty, and I follow this convention in the pages that follow. In addition, I have set biblical passages and lines of special note in italics.

Section I

THE OLD TESTAMENT

This is the bulk of the Bible. About 1,200 of the 1,500 total pages. It starts with the creation of the universe and runs up to just before the arrival of Jesus Christ. It covers the history, lifestyle, laws, and customs of the Jewish people, also known as the Hebrews. The first five chapters are called the Penta-teuch (Penta'-toooook), which means "five scrolls." Jews call this part the Law or Torah. The Jews' name for God is Yahweh, but he answers to God or Lord. These first five chapters hold many of the stories that you'll hear referenced often.

1

Book of Genesis

The Creation Story

Famous quote alert: "*In the beginning God created the heavens and the earth.*" This project took seven days.

On day one God said, "'*Let there be light*'; *and there was light. And God saw that the light was good.*" So he went ahead and made day and night.

On day two He made heaven and earth. Day three, dry land and water. Day four, the sun, moon, and stars. Day five, fish, birds, and sea monsters, which he told to "*Be fruitful and multiply.*"

On day six, God created land beasts, cattle, and "*man in His own image and likeness.*" God put man in charge of all the animals. "You da Man" (not actual Bible quote).

Then came day seven. It had been a pretty busy week, so God rested. That's why religions of the Judeo-Christian tradition make a big deal either about Sunday or the Jewish Sabbath (which overlaps Friday and Saturday—go figure).

The Garden of Eden

Some more details on man's story are provided. In case you were wondering, God scooped up some dust from the ground and breathed life into it from His own nostrils and it became man. That evening, God planted a garden and told man to work there. It was paradise with plenty to eat, but there was one condition: Don't eat the apple from the *Tree of Knowledge of Good and Evil*. Why not? Just because. No really, why? "If you do you shall die." So there.

The first man was named Adam. God let Adam give names to all the animals. Before long, Adam got lonely and was tired of farming all by himself. So God decided to make him a female helper, Eve. Here's how that went down. God caused a deep sleep to fall upon Adam, then took out, like surgically removed, one of Adam's ribs and used it to make Eve.

Once Adam recovered from his rib-ectomy, life in the Garden of Eden couldn't have been better. Adam and his woman were even "naked and not ashamed."

Then, one day, along comes a serpent (snake) who starts talking to Eve. The snake asks her about the forbidden fruit of the Tree of Knowledge and Eve explains the one condition. The crafty snake responds by telling her that's a load of bull and she can eat the fruit. So airheaded Eve does it and then brings Adam an apple and lets him eat it too!

This is the beginning of the recurrent Bible theme that women are trouble, and that man continually breaks the rules of God.

That afternoon, God is strolling through the Garden of Eden and gets wind of what's happened. He has the first of many major temper tantrums of biblical proportions! He confronts Adam, who blames Eve, who blames the snake. God says something to the effect of, "Okay beotches, you're all going down!"

He tells the snake it will be forced to crawl on its belly in the dirt forever and people will hate it. Eve and all women are cursed with severe pain during childbirth. As for Adam and all of mankind? You will work your butts off and have lousy farming land and then die. "*You are dust and to dust you shall return.*" Then God basically says, "Now, everybody get the hell out of the Garden of Eden. You're all banished. Oh and by the way, from now on you'll have to make clothes because you're embarrassed to be naked. Ha!"

Cain and Abel

The bad reality show continues. The couple moves East of Eden. Eve gives birth to two sons, Cain and Abel. Cain is the first born, grows crops, and is sort of a jerk. Abel is nice and raises sheep. One day it's time to bring offerings to God. Cain brings Him a fruit platter from his farm. Abel brings a plump sheep. God the Lord happens to really like sheep and is impressed with Abel. Not so much with Cain's gift. God's like, "Oh man, not fruit again. I had a bad experience with that apple in the not-so-distant past."

Cain is jealous and ticked off at Abel. Later, he invites Abel out into a field. Cain then hits Abel in the head with a rock, killing him dead right there! The world's first homicide.

God comes by and asks Cain, "Where's your bro Abel?" To which Cain responds, "I don't know, what *am I my brother's keeper* or something?" It doesn't take God long to figure things out, and He has another conniption fit. Cain is cursed and the land is made even less fertile. Cain wanders the earth, surprisingly finds a wife, and they start squirting out kids.

Adam and Eve eventually have another son (Seth) and start producing generations. Adam ends up living 930 years before dying. Everyone seems to have exceptionally long lifespans. Methuselah breaks the record at 969 years! Finally God intervenes and puts a limit at 120 years.

Noah and the Great Flood

Humans are taking over the earth and behaving badly. Trying to manage them is a full-time job for God. He starts to have second thoughts about ever creating man. When He looks down on earth, He only sees one righteous person, Noah. Bumming out, God cooks up a plan.

God decides to destroy almost all living things with a torrential flood. He tells Noah to start making a big boat out of gopherwood. It's called an ark. God gives very specific instructions for the ark, which is to be three levels, have doors and a roof, and be 300 *cubits* long. Other dimensions are given in cubits too. (A cubit is about a yard or meter.) God feels he has to micromanage these disappointing humans.

He tells Noah the flood is coming and makes a deal (known as a *covenant*). Noah can bring his whole extended family, food, seven pairs of all clean animals (not specified which), and a male and female pair of every other animal, including birds. (But not fish because they should be fine.) Noah agrees.

God then sends rain upon the world for 40 days and 40 nights, causing the Great Flood. No tsunami warning is given. Noah's ark floats perfectly, while all creatures not on board are drowned. The waters recede and Noah's passengers exit the ark. Noah promptly builds an altar and sacrifices all the clean animals as burnt offerings to God. (Maybe not the best idea given the recent extinction?) But God likes the gesture and tells everyone once again to *"Be fruitful and multiply"* and repopulate the earth. The aroma of the burnt offerings makes God doubt His actions and He gets mildly depressed. So God makes another covenant promising never to destroy everything again and creates the rainbow as a future reminder to make the rain stop at a reasonable time.

Trouble starts up again pretty soon with Noah's sons. The youngest one, Japeth, and the whole land of Canaan are cursed to become slaves to the other brothers.

Noah, who was 601 years old at the time of the flood, lives until age 950. (I guess the set limit was lifted for him.)

Tower of Babel
Tribes are growing and settling different areas. Back then, everyone spoke the same language and there weren't many words available anyway.

Soon enough, one tribe (probably the Babylonians) invented bricks and decided to build a tall tower to reach the heavens. "Everyone will think we're so cool! We can put it on YouTube and Facebook someday."

God is not amused at all by this project. So He comes down to check out the tower. He decides that man is getting a little too uppity and could use a smackdown.

He halts construction, scatters the misbehaving tribe all across the planet, and confuses their speech into many different languages so they can't communicate and start another disrespectful project like this again.

God says, "Hah, now I have a name for your stupid tower, the *Tower of Babel*! Buwah ha hah!"

Lot and His Dysfunctional Family

The Bible then cranks out lists of boring genealogies about people you don't know. Arpachshad begat Shelah, Peleg fathered Reu', etc. Until we get to two brothers, Abraham and Lot.

Both brothers are rich with slaves, herds of animals, wives, and bling. God tells them to pack everything up and He'll show them some real estate and they'll become great nations. The brothers jump at the chance.

Unfortunately, their entourages aren't getting along, so Lot relocates his group over to the wicked towns of Sodom and Gomorrah, where the city dwellers are practicing homosexuals.

Unknown to Lot, God has sent two badass angels to prepare Sodom and Gomorrah for destruction. The two handsome angels show up at Lot's place on the outskirts of Sodom. Lot invites them in for dinner and drinks.

The out-of-control gay guys of Sodom surround Lot's house and demand he give them the two hot angels for a wild homosexual orgy.

Lot, being a reasonable dude, instead offers the gay crowd his two virgin daughters, "Do with them what you please, just leave my handsome dinner guests alone."

The angry gays scream, "You idiot, we don't want your daughters. We're gay, we want the beefy calendar boys. Don't you know, this town invented sodomy!"

Lot is befuddled. Finally the angels take control. They pull Lot inside and say, "Get your family out of here. Flee for your lives. We are going to kick some ass here. Just don't look back. It's going to get ugly fast!"

Lot resists but eventually runs away with his family.

The angels of the Lord rain down fire and brimstone, annihilating everything and everybody in Sodom and its sister city Gomorrah. This may have been the origin of the term "Flaming queens."

On the way out of town, Lot's disobedient wife just has to not follow directions. She turns around to look at the action and is instantly turned into a *pillar of salt*! Some girls never learn.

In a weird postscript, Lot brings his remaining family to live in a cave. His two daughters complain, "We'll never meet any decent guys here. And that last town certainly didn't have any prospects." So they get Lot drunk on wine two nights in a row and "lay with him." That's Bible-speak for have sex. (Same as "he knew them.") As a result, they both have sons who then start different tribes. Kinky.

Abraham

Lot's brother Abraham fared even better. God had big plans for Abe—if he proved worthy. Abraham would become the father of the Jewish nation.

God sent Abraham and his wagon train on a few wild goose chases. First to Egypt where he had some run-ins with the king (Pharaoh). Then to a bunch of other places in the Middle East, always promising him land and many descendants. God is quoted as promising Abraham and his clan all the land between the Nile River in Egypt to the Euphrates River in Iraq. (This is still the source of much controversy in present-day

Israel and surrounding areas.)

God made a covenant guaranteeing these things to Abraham and the Jews. They would be God's *Chosen People*. But Abraham had to jump through many hoops. For example, every male, including the slaves, would have to be circumcised as a sign of the bargain. Abraham said, "No problem," and started cutting off foreskins that same day. Plus there'd be a lot of wandering through the desert, sacrifices, rules, and tests.

Isaac

Abraham was performing well and God rewarded him and his previously childless wife, Sarah, with a son named Isaac.

The most dramatic test comes when Isaac is a young lad. God tells Abraham to take Isaac on a field trip into the mountains, where Abraham must make an altar, kill Isaac, and barbecue him as a burnt offering to God. Straightforward enough.

Remarkably, Abraham starts the three-day donkey trip, gets everything prepared at the altar, starts a fire, ties up Isaac, and puts him on the grill. Isaac starts to ask some basic questions. Abraham responds by raising up a knife to slaughter Isaac! At the last second, an angel of God yells to Abraham to stop, saying he has passed the test of faith and has proven that he truly "*Fears God.*" Abe is so happy he grabs a goat and burns it instead of Issac. Praise the Lord!

For this display, God gives Abraham "more descendants than stars in the sky and sand on the beach" (and of course the previously promised real estate in Palestine).

Isaac gets years of therapy.

Esau and Jacob

Isaac grows up and marries Rebekah, who turns out to be barren, which is Bible-speak for unable to have children. God felt a little bad for Isaac, so He threw him a bone and let Rebekah conceive and deliver twin boys, Esau and Jacob. Esau was slightly older, very hairy, and a good hunter. Jacob was more of a nerd who mostly stayed inside tents.

There is some family drama when Rebekah and her favorite son, Jacob, trick the aging and blind Isaac into giving his blessing to Jacob, instead of the eldest son, Esau. Jacob impersonates the hairy Esau by wearing animal skins, thus stealing the blessing.

Jacob goes off and becomes successful, gets married, rips off his father-in-law's animal herds, talks with God all the time, and sojourns around the territories.

God meets with Jacob and promises him the land of his father Isaac and grandfather Abraham. God then changes Jacob's name to *Israel*. Today, this provides more "evidence" that the land of the ancient Hebrews clearly belongs to Israel.

Joseph and the 12 Tribes of Israel

This story was the basis of the Broadway play, *Joseph and the Amazing Technicolor Dream Coat*.

Jacob, now named Israel, had 12 sons. His favorite was the youngest, Joseph. Joseph's eleven brothers noticed this and were highly jealous. Instead of playing it cool, Joseph really started to rub it in. When he was 17, he began to tell the others about dreams he had where all the brothers and even his parents would bow down to him, and Joseph would reign over them.

This is not the way to win friends. The brothers concocted a plan to kill Joseph, throw him in a pit, and tell their dad that a wild beast had eaten him.

One brother, Reuben (whose name will eventually become associated with a sandwich), convinces them not to kill Joseph, "Let's just throw him in the pit." The others agree and toss Joseph in. Then they tell Israel the wild beast story.

Some foreigners happen by, find Joseph, pull him out of the hole, and sell him to some other travelers.

Joseph ends up in Egypt, where he is sold again, but he becomes successful as a house manager for his new owner. Some domestic canoodling occurs with the owner's wife, and Joe is sent to prison. In jail, he gains acclaim as a dream interpreter and luckily gets a chance to interpret the Pharaoh's dream. Joseph nails it and the Pharoah appoints him manager of Egypt. Joseph stockpiles grain because he predicts a famine is coming and saves the day. During the famine, his father, Israel, sends the eleven brothers to Egypt to get grain. When they arrive they don't realize the bossman is their brother. Joseph recognizes them and tools them around for a while, locking them in prison. Then he sends them home with food and money. Eventually, Joseph reveals his identity and has the brothers bring dad to Egypt, where he sets them all up with good land.

Joseph then enslaves the Egyptians and makes them pay a 20 percent tax. Israel dies and the brothers scatter to become the *12 tribes of Israel*.

2

Book of Exodus

Our story picks up with the 12 sons of Israel (Jacob) being fruitful and multiplying. In time, Joseph and his brothers die and a new Pharoah takes over in Egypt. (No explanation of how the Egyptians got out of slavery and took over again is given.) The new Pharaoh doesn't like all these Hebrew tribes breeding, so he decides to enslave them. The Pharaoh also decrees that all Hebrew newborn boys shall be thrown into the Nile River. (The girls can live because nobody cares about girls anyway.)

Moses
Instead of throwing her baby boy in the river, one Jewish mother decides to hide her son in a basket made of bullrushes down by the river bank. The Pharoah's daughter finds the baby, adopts him, and names him Moses. When Moses grows up he kills an Egyptian who was beating up a Hebrew. When word gets around, Moses flees Egypt and marries into a good family with livestock, but he is still distressed at the plight of his

fellow Hebrews working as slaves back in Egypt.

One day, Moses is out tending his flock around Mount Horeb, when God appears to him in the form of a *burning bush*. They chat a little and God suggests Moses go lead the oppressed Hebrews, the children of Israel, out of Egypt and deliver them to *a land flowing with milk and honey*.

Moses is a little skeptical. He questions, "In case anyone asks, who should I say sent me?" And God says, "Just call me *I am who am.*"

This riddle did not make Moses feel any more confident. So God gave him three miracle tricks to perform if needed, the most famous being turning a snake into a stick! This stick is the "*Rod of God*" or walking staff that Moses is usually pictured holding in paintings.

Plagues of Egypt

Moses, along with his brother, Aaron, go back to Egypt and meet with the Pharoah. They say, "Mr. Pharoah, *let my people go.*" And the Pharaoh responds, "Ahh, no." Then increases the workload and beatings of the Hebrews, just for asking.

Moses reports back to God, "Excuse me, I am who am, that did not go well." God says again how he promised the Hebrews land in the Levant and sends Moses back to get them out of Egypt. "Go do the tricks I showed you earlier." So Moses and Aaron go back to the Pharoah and throw the stick down and it turns into a snake! Ho-hum, the Egyptian magicians can do that too. Okay, Moses then turns the water of the Nile into blood. Shazam! Still no movement from the Pharaoh: "Big deal, we can do that too." Moses tells the Pharaoh to think it over.

Seven days later and still nothing. So God gets serious and has Moses unleash a series of plagues on Egypt. Frogs come up out of the river and into people's beds. Swarms of gnats and flies infest everybody's houses. The Pharaoh is temporarily impressed. After each plague he says, "Okay, you can lead your people away." But when the plagues recede, he changes his mind and keeps the Hebrews enslaved.

The Pharaoh's playing hardball like a car salesman. So then come plagues of diseased Egyptian livestock, hailstorms, locusts, and darkness. Every time the same response from the Pharaoh, "Oh, okay, you win, make it stop." Followed by, "No, the Hebrews really have to stay."

Passover
This is a long story. Finally God has one more plague up his sleeve. He tells Moses to instruct the Hebrews to get ready on the tenth day of a certain month because there's going to be a massive beat down of the Egyptians. God's going to show up at midnight and kill every firstborn son, including the Pharaoh's (and every firstborn of cattle too)!

To protect the Jewish firstborns, each family is told to slaughter an unblemished lamb and smear some of its blood above their doorways. Then cook and eat the lamb along with some unleavened bread and bitter herbs. Lots of specific instructions follow.

At the appointed hour, God shows up and smites every firstborn in Egypt, but he "*passes over*" the Hebrew houses that have the secret blood smear sign over the doorways.

This catastrophe works and the Pharaoh gives in. Modern-day Jews commemorate this ritual every year, known as the feast of Passover. Moses and Aaron successfully lead the Hebrews out of Egypt.

Parting the Red Sea

God helps lead the group along by a *pillar of cloud* during the day and a *pillar of fire* by night. He guides them over the scenic route to the Red Sea and has them camp there. God and Moses scheme together because God still has some wrong sauce to lay on the Pharaoh.

Before long, the Pharaoh and Egyptians start to miss having all those Hebrew slaves around. So they mobilize the army and 600 chariots to go reclaim their slaves.

The Hebrews see them coming and are terrified. God puts the pillar of cloud in the way to provide cover while Moses raises his rod and God sends a strong wind to separate the waters of the Red Sea. Moses leads the Hebrews through the pathway created between the two halves of the sea, while God watches from the pillar of fire. When the Pharaoh and his army follow them through the gap between the two parts of the sea, their chariot wheels get stuck in the seafloor mud and they become trapped. Moses raises his rod again and the two halves of the Red Sea slam back together, drowning all the Egyptians and their horses. Dang!

Everybody then knew beyond a shadow of a doubt, that the God of the Hebrews was the real deal.

Desert Happenings

Moses and Aaron continue to lead the Jews through the desert and wilderness, sojourning around for 40 years. As you can imagine, there was a lot of grousing and moaning: "Are we there yet?" "I'm thirsty." "There are no restaurants anywhere." People also start slacking off about obeying rules and do things like not rest on the Sabbath. Moses keeps relaying complaints to God, saying, "Hey, the people are crabby; some of these complainers are going to stone me to death down here." God intervenes multiple times by sending quail birds over to be barbecued, raining down special bread—*"Manna from heaven"*—just about daily, and, the big crowd pleaser, letting Moses get some street cred by striking a rock with his rod and causing water to flow out like a fire hydrant!

This one went over well and restored calm to the masses.

The Sacred Covenant

God and Moses were now on a hot streak. So God commanded Moses to come up to the top of Mount Sinai to talk strategy. Moses *went to the mountaintop* and met with God, while the people of Israel waited below. Moses stayed up there 40 days and 40 nights. All the people down below could see were clouds and flashes of lightning, interspersed with rolls of thunder and the occasional startling trumpet blast.

Negotiations went well and a deal was struck between God and Moses. It was called *the sacred covenant* and sealed with blood.

In the covenant, God again promised the Hebrews all the land from the Red Sea to the Sea of the Philistines and from the wilderness all the way to the Euphrates River. God would occasionally send hornets to drive out the local tribes, so the Hebrews could slowly take over all the land. (Are you starting to see why the Middle East is still such a mess?)

Ten Commandments

In return for this *promised land*, the people agree to live by the *Ten Commandments*, which God gave Moses, along with pages and pages of "ordinances" detailing lots and lots of rules. The Ten Commandments are: (1) I am the Lord your God, who brought you out of the land of Egypt, out of the house of bondage. You shall have no other gods before me; (2) You shall not make a graven image or likeness of other gods. You shall not bow down to them or serve them; for I the Lord your God am a jealous God; (3) You shall not take the name of the Lord your God in vain; (4) Remember the Sabbath day to keep it holy; (5) Honor your father and your mother; (6) You shall not kill; (7) You shall not commit adultery; (8) You shall not steal; (9) You shall not bear false witness against your neighbor; (10) You shall not covet your neighbor's house; you shall not covet your neighbor's wife, or his manservant, or his maidservant, or his ox, or his ass, or anything of your neighbor's.

The ordinances give commonsense rules for all kinds of things like: You shall not permit a sorceress to live. Whoever sacrifices to any God, save to the Lord only, shall be utterly destroyed. You shall not boil a kid (young goat) in its mother's milk. Whoever curses his father or his mother shall be put to death. Whoever lies with a beast shall be put to death. When you buy a Hebrew slave, he shall serve six years and in the seventh he shall go free. If an ox gores a slave, the owner shall give to the slave's master 30 shekels of silver, and the ox shall be stoned. When a man strikes a slave, male or female, with a rock and the slave dies, he shall be punished. But if the slave survives a day or two, he is not to be punished. Okay, got that? It's the word of the Lord.

Wait, we're not done. Then God gave Moses excruciatingly detailed instructions on how to build an ark (box) in which to keep a copy of the signed deal. The special box is called the *Ark of the Covenant*. Plus, specifications for a mobile tabernacle to keep the ark in—tent poles, veils, garments, jewels, gold and silver decorations, tables, altars, lamps and furnishings, curtains with loops and clasps, screens, pillars, turbans, girdles, priestly uniforms with insignia, robes, gold chains, caps, measurements, a bronze sink for washing, and directions for sacrifices. Oh, and also how to take a census. And collect atonement money.

"Whoa," Moses said, "How am I going remember all that?" So God scrawled notes on some stone tablets using his own finger, *the finger of God*. Powerful.

Okay, we're all good here. *Moses came down from the mountain.*

The Golden Calf and Broken Tablets

Well, wouldn't you know, Aaron and the people of Israel couldn't even behave for 40 days, even with those unpredictable trumpet blasts. While Moses was gone they melted down their gold jewelry, used their graving tools, and formed a *Golden Calf* icon to worship. Yes, a *graven image*! Complete with sacrifices and dancing!

When Moses saw this, he went ballistic. He threw the stone tablets down, breaking them into smithereens; called Aaron an unprintable name; ordered 3,000 men killed; ground up the calf, mixed it with water, and made all the idiots drink it. Plus, the next day he had to tell God about it!

Since this was before anger management classes were

invented, God reacted in his usual way and sent a plague. Then he summoned Moses back up Mount Sinai.

Rewrite

For the next 40 days and 40 nights (and a bunch of Bible pages), God and Moses went over every stinking detail again. They rewrote the covenant and Ten Commandments on two more stone tablets and Moses *came down again from the mountaintop.*

This time the people of Israel accepted the deal and started building the ark, tent, tabernacle, and all the uniforms and stuff, just how God wanted it, in excruciating detail.

When everything was done, God enjoyed hanging out in the tabernacle. He'd show his presence by covering the tabernacle with a cloud whenever He was in there during the day, and with fire by night. Then He'd lift the cloud when it was time to move the *chosen people* onward again, toward the *promised land.*

3

Book of Leviticus

You won't hear many heartwarming stories from this book of the Bible. In fact, it should make any halfway reasonable person question the premise that the Bible is divinely inspired.

Leviticus is a laundry list of God telling Moses more rules and instructions for living. Important things like exactly how to perform burnt offerings, sin offerings, guilt offerings, peace offerings, even cereal offerings. How to choose and flay an animal for sacrifice, ring off a turtledove's head, prepare goat entrails, sprinkle blood. If you can't afford a lamb, two young pigeons may be substituted. Also lengthy discussions of which animals to sacrifice to atone for which sins. More rituals for a yearly day of atonement are described. This event is still commemorated by Jews on the tenth day of the seventh month and is known as Yom Kippor.

Clean versus Unclean

Then we hear how the priests will determine what's clean or unclean. Women: unclean for seven days during menstruation and of course anyone who touches her during that time is contaminated. Men: unclean after emitting semen, until a bath that night. Animals: no eating unclean beasts like swine, camel, hare, or the rock badger. If you touch a carcass of these you'll become unclean. Sea creatures with fins or scales are okay but anything else is an abomination. Birds, insects, swarming things also are abominations. Too bad for the eagle, owl, stork, mouse, weasel, and gecko. But there is some good news, you can eat winged insects that have four feet. Yum.

Disease Management

Human afflictions are also categorized as clean or unclean. Some burns and baldness can be clean. But leprosy, pus drainage, and most itching diseases are unclean and need special sacrifices.

Bad Sex and Gays

Next we are told which sexual relationships are forbidden. The usual ones like incest are banned. The modern-day religious denunciation of homosexuality comes from this passage: "*You shall not lie with a man as with a woman; it is an abomination. And the penalty is death by stoning for both partners.*"

Odds and Ends

Here are some other tidbits: Don't burn your children as sacrifices to other gods. Don't cut the hair on your temples or trim your beard. (This is the reason you see Orthodox Jews with curly sideburns, beards, and hats.) Don't turn to wizards or practice witchcraft. Penalty: stoning to death. Same punishment for adultery for both offenders. In the case of bestiality, man or woman and the beast are killed. If you work on the Sabbath, you'll be destroyed. We even get some real estate law: If a man sells a house in a walled city, he may redeem it within a year after its sale.

Monetary values for humans are given in shekels of silver. Males aged 20–60 are worth the most, 50 shekels; women max out at 30 shekels. Formulas are given for other ages.

Comic Relief

We are given a story to break up the piling on of rules. A half Egyptian boy is going around camp cursing and blaspheming God's name. They bring the troubled lad to Moses who locks him up until he hears from God. Soon enough, God decides to have the foul-mouthed kid stoned to death by the entire congregation. Curses!

An Eye for an Eye

Here comes the granddaddy of all Old Testament Bible rules: "When a man causes disfigurement of his neighbor, as he has done it shall be done to him, fracture for fracture, *eye for an eye, tooth for a tooth.*"

What If We Don't?

God wraps up Leviticus with a barrage of hurt if the rules aren't followed, the covenant is broken, or ordinances are ignored. You thought plagues were bad? How about sudden terror, consumption, fever that burns your eyes out, wild beasts eating your children, cities being laid waste, vengeance, fury, stalking, and the promise to "never again smell your pleasing odors."

Stick with the program and you'll beat your enemies, have enough to eat, get the promised land, and enjoy the milk and honey.

4

Book of Numbers

Remember the census God said he wanted? Well here it is. A tally of how many males over 20 years of age, in each of the 12 tribes of Israel, still sojourning around in the wilderness. In case you were wondering, the total was "603,550."

Also, God gives instructions on where each tribe is supposed to camp. The tribe of Levi is put in charge of moving and setting up the fancy tabernacle. All lepers or members with unclean discharges are thrown out of camp. More ancient laws, ordinances, sacrifices, instructions for priests, guidance on how to curse your wife for infidelity, and chats between Moses and God are painstakingly recorded.

The people suddenly get cranky, "We want meat. We're sick of this manna from the sky stuff." God is predictably not amused, but orders in some barbecued quails. Which satisfies the folk for a while.

The people of Israel lose a battle against another tribe. More whining ensues, "We want to go back to Egypt." "Slavery wasn't all that bad." "Where's the milk and honey? Whaa whaa."

Moses is in constant crisis management. God demands more burnt offerings and financial donations in the form of *tithes*. Aaron "*breathes his last breath.*" In the Bible, when someone close to you dies, you show grief by (ripping) *rending your garments* and covering yourself in *sackcloth and ashes*. Sackcloth is coarse burlap made from goats' hair. Ashes are what's leftover in your fireplace.

More battles against other tribes are described, with the Hebrews winning, then promptly slaughtering all the losers, including women and children, but happily giving any virgin girls to the soldiers! Nice.

The people of Israel get ready to cross the Jordan River at Jericho, fight the Canaanites and other abominable tribes, and take their territory as the promised land.

Overall, nothing quotable.

5

Book of Deuteronomy

Moses gives some long speeches rehashing everything from the previous two chapters. He adds a warning: When you cross the Jordan and defeat other tribes, whatever you do, don't adopt their gods, and remember to stone to death any prophets or dreamers who recommend other gods.

Most rules are repeats but some new ones appear: How to properly take concubines, hang people, keep slaves, and get divorced—oh, and please remember to poop outside the camp in a hole dug with a stick and cover it because God walks around inside the camp. (I'm not kidding.) Punishment for children who don't obey their parents is death by stoning. No bastards or men with crushed testicles are allowed in the tabernacle.

Glad we got that settled.

The Mountaintop
The grand finale of Moses' speech is when he says he's now 120 years old and slowing down. He tells the people of Israel

that Joshua will be leading them across the Jordan River and finding the promised land. God then calls Moses up onto another mountain, Mount Nebo, where He says, "I've got good news and bad news." The good news is He shows Moses the promised land, which is visible from the mountaintop. But the bad news is Moses won't be going there, and Moses dies.

Fun fact: This is where Reverend Martin Luther King, Jr., got his material for his final speech in 1968, "I've Been to the Mountaintop." " ... And He's allowed me to go up to the mountain. And I've looked over. And I've seen the Promised Land. I may not get there with you. But I want you to know tonight, that we, as a people, will get to the Promised Land!"

6

Book of Joshua

Prepare for Holy War as God's chosen people claim the land He promised them. God tells Moses' successor, Joshua, to get ready to rumble.

Parting of the Jordan
Since the parting of the Red Sea by Moses was such a crowd pleaser, God lets Joshua part the Jordan River! The people of Israel follow their priests carrying the Ark of the Covenant right across without even getting wet. Once on the other side, they make camp and plan the siege of Jericho.

Battle of Jericho
God gives Joshua a special war plan to conquer the walled city of Jericho. Every day for seven days, the people of Israel march around the perimeter outside the city walls carrying the Ark of the Covenant and blowing seven ram's horn trumpets. Each day they walk around one additional time. On the seventh day, they march around seven times, blow the trumpets, and on the

seventh blow, everyone lets out a really loud shout. The noise topples the city's walls and the Hebrews are victorious! *And the walls came tumbling down.* Then they use their swords to wipe out the city's population—and its animals too. Oh snap.

Further Conquests

Joshua then leads the Hebrews throughout the Middle East, sacking cities, slaying kings and tribes, and gobbling up real estate.

They lose one skirmish but win everything else. They grab the land of the Hittites, Amorites, Canaanites, Perizzites, Hivites, and Jebusites. (Curiously, Parasites are not mentioned.) In some places they can't drive out all the inhabitants, so some non-Jews remain (causing trouble even then). Modern-day hot spots like Jerusalem and Gaza are notable examples.

Joshua then parcels out all the conquered territory among the tribes of Israel for them to hold forever and pass down to their descendants.

7

Books of Judges 1 and 2

After Joshua dies, other leaders emerge, known as judges. They lead the twelve tribes through more conquests, violence, and drama. Most are victories with God's direct assistance, but sometimes the Hebrews slip up and start worshipping false gods again. The real God remains jealous and always reacts badly. Sometimes a plague is sent, sometimes they're temporarily enslaved until they come to their senses and reject the other gods.

Most of these judges you've never heard of and never will. But one is famous.

Samson and Delilah

Samson was a leader of Israel who became a celebrity for his feats of strength. He wasn't good in relationships, visited hookers, and was always getting into brawls with the Philistines. One day he met and fell in love with the beautiful Delilah. The Philistine leaders were really sick of Samson, so they made Delilah an offer: Find out the source of Samson's strength, and we'll give you 1,100 pieces of silver. She says, "I'm more of a golddigger, but silver, okay, sure."

So Delilah engages in some pillow talk and Samson tells her a fake story about a special rope being able to contain him. Delilah reports this to the Philistines, who jump Samson and tie him up with the special rope. Samson easily breaks the rope and goes back to Delilah.

She really wants the silver, so she asks him again. "Poopsie, what's your secret strength source? Is it steroids?" Samson tells Delilah another bogus story with the same exact result.

Same story occurs yet again but amazingly, this time dumbass Samson tells her the true source of his strength: It's his long hair that has never been cut! So Delilah tells the Philistines and collects the payoff. Later, while Samson is sleeping in her lap, she has a barber come in and shave Samson's head. When he later wakes up, she busts his chops a little and finds that Samson truly is weak. The Philistines rush in and gouge Samson's eyes out and throw him in a Gaza jail.

While incarcerated, Samson's hair starts to grow back. The Philistines are having a big party to honor their false god and, much to the delight of the enormous crowd, trot Samson out to taunt him publically. They place Samson between the main pillars of their big entertainment hall and convention center. The now-blind Samson prays for one more burst of strength. He puts each hand on a pillar and pushes them over, collapsing the entire building and killing himself and over 3,000 Philistines! And that's the truth.

8

Book of Ruth

Nothing quotable here. Move along.

9

Books of Samuel 1 and 2

Both books of Samuel serve up beheadings, *beating plowshares into swords,* rape, more politics, war, people being smote, bad behavior, rending of garments, plagues, and pestilence. But we also get two famous stories about David.

David and Goliath
Saul is the current king of Israel and he's mixing it up again with the Philistines. Both armies are lined up for battle when the Philistines send out a giant warrior named Goliath of Gath. Goliath yells to the Hebrews, "Attention you wimps, send out your champion and we'll go one on one to the death for all the marbles. If I win, you'll become our slaves and vice versa."

The Israeli army is petrified and no one volunteers until King Saul's armor bearer, David, comes forward. David is a young sheepherder who plays music on the lyre and is great at calming down Saul.

King Saul says to David, "You're nuts. That dude is huge." But David retorts, "It's all cool. God is on my side." Saul says okay, dresses David in a full suit of armor, and gives him a big sword. Young David can hardly move and says, "This will never work. I'll just stroll out there naked with a slingshot and baggie holding five smooth stones." (This was the inspiration for Michelangelo's famous statue of David.)

The ultimate fighting match gets under way. Goliath, using sword and spear, charges right at David. Little David runs away and whips a rock with his sling, nailing Goliath right in the head, killing him instantly. Then David grabs Goliath's sword, stabs the giant, and, just to be sure, lops his head off.

The Philistines freak out and run away. Some are heard to mutter, "Lucky shot, David."

Needless to say, the people of Israel are thrilled, and King Saul gives David one of his best-looking daughters to marry. A bunch of drama unfolds, foreign and domestic. David eventually becomes king, acquiring concubines and livin' large.

David and Bathsheba

King David's walking around on the palace roof one day peeping around, when he spots a beautiful woman taking a bath. Her name is Bathsheba, the wife of Uriah.

David sends a royal messenger over to invite her to "hang out." Bathsheba hooks up with David and gets pregnant. It's like a biblical soap opera.

King David hatches a plan to get rid of Bathsheba's husband, Uriah. He tells his generals to put Uriah on the front lines of the daily battle, then have the other soldiers quietly fall back, leaving Uriah out front like a sitting duck. The plan works and Uriah gets speared.

David sends for Bathsheba and marries her. God is ticked off and makes their son die, but He lets them have another son, named Solomon, who becomes the next king—after more family drama of course.

10

Books of Kings 1 and 2

King David dies and Solomon takes the throne. God asks Solomon what gift he would like best? To which Solomon gives the right answer: "Give me an understanding mind between good and evil." God is impressed and things go well—for a while.

Wisdom of Solomon
Right off the bat, two harlots come in asking King Solomon to settle a domestic dispute. They live together and each has a newborn son. One hefty harlot rolls over in bed and crushes her kid; then before the other harlot wakes up, switches the dead kid for the live one. A catfight ensues with both moms claiming the living son belongs to them. Can you please solve this harlot controversy King Solomon?

Solomon says, "That's easy," and calls for a sharp sword. "Divide the living kid in two and give half to each mom. One mom says, "Sounds good." The other says, "No way. Don't do it. You can give the whole kid to her." To which Solomon declares, "That's the real mom—the one who won't let me carve the kid up—give it to her."

When people hear about this, Solomon's approval rating shoots up. This begins a golden age of unity between the tribes. Solomon even made peace with Egypt by marrying one of the Pharaoh's daughters. He amassed great riches, prosperity reigned, and the people were happy. King Solomon also went on a building campaign. He ordered rock quarried, constructed walls around his capital, Jerusalem (the City of David, his father), made a Hall of the Throne, a Hall of Judgment, and an assembly hall. A fleet of ships was commissioned, and the army supplied with brand-spanking-new chariots. Best of all, he built a permanent temple for the Ark of the Covenant to reside in. No more hauling it around under a tent. The awesome *Temple of Solomon* was built in Jerusalem and constructed of the finest cedars of Lebanon and bronze. This was done with slave labor from tribes they couldn't fully annihilate. No bother. Things were going great.

So great, that Solomon forgot one of God's rules. He collected 700 wives and 300 concubines from around the realm. God had warned, "Don't marry outside your religion. These wives will get you to worship their false gods. And you know I sort of have a thing about that."

And sure enough, Solomon did start to accept those other gods his wily wives introduced him to. So the real God has another meltdown and raises up rivals and worst of all, Syrians, and pits them against Israel!

Solomon dies and the whole empire starts to unravel. Splits between tribes, bad kings, competition, murder, and lots of stories you'll never hear about—except one.

Jezebel and Ahab

One of the string of lousy rulers was King Ahab. He married Jezebel, who worshiped one of the fake other gods, called Ba'al. If that wasn't bad enough, she also had a neighbor who owned a vineyard that Ahab coveted. In order to cheer Ahab up, Jezebel trumps up charges of "cursing God" against the neighbor. She has the poor guy stoned to death, and gives Ahab the vineyard. Getting the vineyard cheers Ahab up, but God has to ruin the party and rain more evil down upon everyone. God curses them, saying, "Dogs will eat their corpses." Nice. Even today the name Jezebel is synonymous with an evil woman.

Things continue to go downhill for the people of Israel. More bad rulers, massacres, and shady dealings abound. Prophets start to appear, performing healing miracles and warning everyone to avoid false gods—all to no avail.

God finally says, "I've had it with you people." He lets the Syrians take some promised land away from the chosen people. Eventually the Babylonians sweep in under their King Nebuchadnezzar, take over everything, sack Jerusalem, and install a local governor, forcing the King of Israel into exile. Take that!

11

Books of Chronicles 1 and 2

A big rehash of history, except whitewashed to make Kings David and Solomon look like superheroes. Contradicts many details of previous books.

12

Books of Ezra,
Nehemiah, and Esther

Exiled Hebrews drift back into Jerusalem and slowly rebuild the temple and city walls, start to follow the rules again, divorce their non-Jewish Gentile wives, collect religious tithes, and face some resistance from the other inhabitants.

13

Book of Job

Job is a "just and blameless man who fears God and turns away from evil." God is understandably quite proud of Job. Satan, the Devil, pipes up and challenges God, "Well of course Job is good, he's got a really cushy life. Take some of his toys away and he'll be cursing God before you know it!"

God takes the bait and starts pulling Job's chain. First, his oxen and asses are stolen. Then his servants are slaughtered, sheep are incinerated by a heavenly thunderbolt, and his kids are killed by a roof collapse caused by a suspicious freak wind.

Job keeps his faith and God thinks He has won the bet against Satan. Then Satan counters, "Not so fast. You still haven't done anything to Job himself."

God pauses and thinks, "That little devil is right. I'll come up with something." So God afflicts Job with loathsome sores from head to toe. And they itch too. The book goes on forever with long poetic speeches and debates, but Job always hangs in there and keeps praising God. Ultimately, God wins the bet and restores Job's fortunes by double. Gee, thanks.

You may hear someone refer to the *"patience of Job,"* and this story is what they mean. It has absolutely nothing to do with Steve Jobs of Apple fame.

14

Book of Psalms

And now for a musical interlude. There are 150 hymns contained in this book. The psalms are the lyrics of religious songs. None have videos. Overall, they are a mixed bag, some good, most not.

The most famous is the 23rd Psalm, which is popular at funerals: "*The Lord is my shepherd, I shall not want; he makes me lie down in green pastures. He leads me beside still waters; he restores my soul. He leads me in paths of righteousness for his name's sake. Even though I walk through the valley of the shadow of death, I fear no evil. For thou art with me; thy rod and thy staff, they comfort me. Thou preparest a table before me in the presence of my enemies; thou anointest my head with oil, my cup overflows. Surely goodness and mercy shall follow me all the days of my life; and I shall dwell in the house of the Lord forever.*"

Many of the songs recount the history and stories presented in the previous chapters.

15

Book of Proverbs

You would think there'd be some useful pearls of wisdom here, but the selection is pretty disappointing. "For the lips of a loose woman drip honey, and her speech is smoother than oil; but in the end she is bitter as wormwood." Hey God, that's slightly hurtful and misogynistic, don't you think?

The poverty stricken don't catch a break either. "The poor is disliked even by his neighbor, but the rich has many friends."

Animals are mentioned: "The horse is made ready for the day of battle, but the victory belongs to the Lord." Some things you may not have known: "He who winks his eyes plans perverse things, he who compresses his lips brings evil to pass." (Sort of makes you wonder what modern people do in Bible study class? "Okay everyone, what is God telling us here?")

There are, however, some helpful tidbits: "He who is slow to anger is better than the mighty. . . . Do not plan evil against your neighbor who dwells trustingly beside you." "A fool takes no pleasure in understanding, but only in expressing his opinions."

And there is one quotable line you may hear some day: "Pride goes before destruction, and a haughty spirit before a fall." This is often paraphrased as: *Pride cometh before a fall.*

16

Book of Ecclesiastes

Notable quote: *"Cast your bread upon the waters, for you may find it after many days."* Often used to justify taking a chance.

The most famous passage is often quoted and set to music. The '60s folk rock band The Byrds had a number one hit with it in 1965, called "Turn! Turn! Turn!" Here's the Bible section: "For everything there is a season, and a time for every matter under heaven: a time to be born, and a time to die; a time to plant, and a time to pluck up what is planted; a time to kill, and a time to heal; a time to break down, and a time to build up; a time to weep, and a time to laugh; a time to mourn, and a time to dance; a time to cast away stones, and a time to gather stones together; a time to embrace, and a time to refrain from embracing; a time to seek, and a time to lose; a time to keep, and a time to cast away; a time to rend, and a time to sew; a time to keep silence, and a time to speak; a time to love, and a time to hate; a time for war, and a time for peace. What gain has the worker from this toil?"

In my humble opinion, The Byrds' version is better.

17

Book of Solomon

For some odd reason, a strange burst of love poems comprises this book. I hate to think it, but this probably represents Bible porn.

"Your rounded thighs are like jewels. . . . Your neck is like an ivory tower. . . . Your two breasts are like two fawns. . . . How graceful are your feet in sandals. . . . Let us go early to the vineyards, and see whether the vines have budded. . . . There I will give you my love." Racy and not safe for work.

18

Books of Isaiah, Jeremiah, Lamentations, and Ezekiel

Back to ancient history. Things generally suck for the Hebrews. Most are in exile, many flirt with false gods, they're ruled over by foreign powers (Babylonians, Assyrians, Persians). More pesky prophets keep yelling at everyone to follow God's rules, get back in line, stop "playing the harlot," and repent, while promising them a savior (*the messiah*).

Being a prophet must have been a competitive occupation. Some of them could really lay it on thick. If you were to recite these colorful rants out loud in public, say anytime after about the 1700s, you'd be sent directly to a mental institution. "Wail, for the day of the Lord is near; as destruction from the Almighty it will come!" "Their infants will be dashed to pieces. . . . And their wives ravished." "Their slain shall be cast out, and the stench of their corpses shall rise." "And the streams of Edom shall be turned to pitch, and their soil to brimstone, her land shall become burning pitch . . . but the hawk and the porcupine shall possess it." " Ruin shall come on you suddenly, of which you know nothing." "Pour out thy wrath upon the nations that know thee not, and upon the peoples that call not on thy name." "I have brought against the mothers of young men a destroyer at noonday." And the often paraphrased, *"How the mighty have fallen!"*

Modern-day descendants of Hebrews, the Jews, are still waiting for the messiah. Those descendants who later became Christians, believe that Jesus Christ (who arrives later in the Bible) is the messiah. Christ actually means messiah or anointed one. It wasn't Jesus' last name. Last names hadn't even come into use yet. Also, contrary to many scholars, his middle initial was not really H.

19

Book of Daniel

This book describes some stories and dreams—some portray the end of the world, or apocalypse, and some are digs at the heathen rulers currently in charge. Daniel is an exiled Hebrew and gains notoriety as an interpreter of dreams for kings (sounds vaguely familiar).

Handwriting on the Wall
Daniel gets his big break during a huge feast being thrown by King Belshazzar. Everyone's drinking wine out of the stolen gold and silver goblets from the sacked temple in Jerusalem. The party is bangin' until the king spots a disembodied hand writing a bizzare message on the wall. The music stops and jaws drop. King B'shaz summons all the enchanters and astrologers to decode the message and promises riches and a share of leadership to the one who can explain it. They all fail except for Daniel. He's the one who can read the handwriting on the wall and it's bad news for anyone who has dishonored the true God of the Hebrews. Daniel is so cool he doesn't even

want the reward. King Belshazzar is mysteriously slain later that night.

The expression, "the handwriting is on the wall," is often used today to mean that some impending misfortune or disaster awaits.

Daniel in the Lions' Den

King Darius of Persia takes over and declares a 30-day suspension of all worship, except worship of himself. The penalty for any violation is being tossed into a den of hungry lions. Daniel, being devoutly religious, defies the order and prays to the true God of Israel. Daniel's dragged before the king and gets whisked into the lions' den. A big rock is then placed across the doorway. King Darius feels sort of bad about this, so the next morning, he goes to the den and yells out, "Hey Daniel, did your God save you from the lions?" Darius is shocked to hear a voice from inside the den, "Damn straight. My God sent an angel who shut the lions' mouths."

King Darius is impressed and releases Daniel, then decrees that all men shall tremble and fear before Daniel's living God. Daniel continues his career of having fantasy dreams. Unfortunately for Daniel and the Hebrews, these are just dreams, and they continue to be ruled by occupying pagan powers on their own promised land.

20

Book of Jonah

Jonah was a reluctant prophet. God told him to go to the big city of Nineveh and tell the residents their behavior was deplorable and God was going to flame them. Jonah thought, "No way I am doing that," and he ran to the coast and got on the first boat out. God, as you can imagine, was not pleased and hurled a great wind and storm upon the sea. Everybody on board the vessel wanted to know who had displeased their God. Jonah the Hebrew got outed as the offender, and the passengers and crew threw his rump overboard.

Jonah and the Whale
The sea calmed down and God sent a "great fish" to swallow Jonah whole! He spent three days and three nights in the belly of the fish, which gave him time to repent. Finally, Jonah agreed to become a prophet and go tell the people to stop worshipping fake gods and idols. So God told the great fish to vomit Jonah back out onto the beach. After drying off, Jonah went to Nineveh and started doing what prophets do.

21

Books of Hosea, Joel, Amos, Obadiah, Micah, Nahum, Habakkuk, Zephaniah, Haggai, Zechariah, and Malachi

The doom and gloom prophets are featured again, but in mercifully shorter chapters. Same old message: "You people suck, you're not following the rules and ordinances, you're worshipping that idiot god Ba'al, that's why everything is going south; better clean up your acts or we'll all get smote."

Fun trivia from Hosea: God tells him to marry a harlot named Gomer. They have two kids and God names them, Not My People and Not Pitied, as in, "I have 'no pity' for all the houses of Israel, they're 'not my people' anymore—I don't really give a goat's ass about them anymore." That is stone cold.

Bad call from Haggai and Zechariah: they pick Zerubbabel, son of a governor of Judah, as the messiah. Like many first-round draft picks, we never hear about Zerubbabel again.

Section II

THE NEW TESTAMENT

The Middle East of the New Testament is now ruled over by the Roman Empire. The Hebrews are still a mess, but they have rebuilt their temple in Jerusalem and have been hounded by a whole series of prophets.

Fast forward to the year 1 AD. The New Testament starts with the life and times of Jesus H. Christ. (Okay, no H, and to review, Christ means messiah, anointed one, or savior.) This section is so important to Christians (followers of Christ), that it includes four versions of the same basic story. These four versions are known as the Gospels, written by Matthew, Mark, Luke, and John. Gospel means "good news." The good news is that God sent his son, Jesus, who Christians believe is also God, to earth as the messiah to give humanity a chance at salvation and everlasting life in heaven.

The rest of the New Testament covers the adventures of Jesus' followers, the Apostles, as they spread the good news and start the early Christian church.

We conclude with a future prediction of the end of the world. It's a lovely feel-good chapter describing the shellacking, violent destruction, and final judgment of mankind, along with the predicted second coming of Jesus.

22

The Gospels
According to Matthew, Mark,
Luke, and John

Each Gospel represents a separate chapter in the Bible. For our purposes, we'll lump them together since they all describe similar stories. There are repetitions, inconsistencies, and omissions, but they're basically the same.

Christmas and the Virgin Birth

Luke's Gospel contains the familiar Christmas story. Matthew has a strange version of it and Mark and John have nothing at all about Jesus' birth.

Here's Luke's story: God's angel, Gabriel, appears to a virgin woman named Mary, and tells her she's going to remain a virgin but become impregnated by the Holy Spirit of God and have a son. She is instructed to name him Jesus and he'll be the son of God, sent to be the messiah. She agrees, *"Behold, I am the handmaiden of the Lord."*

The Roman Emperor, Caesar Augustus, decrees that every man must return to his hometown to be counted in a new census. The virginal but very pregnant Mary is betrothed (engaged) to Joseph, so she goes with him to the town of Bethlehem to be counted. All the hotels are booked, so they stay in an animal stable (manger).

Murphy's Law kicks in and Mary gives birth to baby Jesus and *"wrapped him in swaddling clothes and laid him in a manger."*

Shepherds in a field are approached by an angel who announces, *". . . for to you is born this day in the City of David a Savior, who is Christ the Lord."* Then a heavenly choir bursts forth singing, *"Glory to God in the highest, and on Earth peace among men with whom he is pleased!"*

On the eighth day, Jesus is circumsized. That's it for Luke's Christmas tale. Matthew mentions the *"wise men from the East"* who looked for the newborn king of the Jews. They followed a bright star to a house (not a stable) where they found Mary and Jesus. They gave gifts of *"gold, frankincense, and myrrh."*

Matthew's Gospel traces Jesus' lineage back to King David. Luke takes it all the way back to Adam!

John the Baptist

Around the same time as Mary's *immaculate conception*, the angel Gabriel appeared to her relative Elizabeth. Gabriel said that the older and barren Elizabeth will have a son and name him John. He'll be filled with the Holy Spirit and prepare the population for the arrival of the Lord.

John is born and when he grows up, he moves into the wilderness and eats locusts and honey. One day God appears and tells him to go to the Jordan River, baptize people with water, forgive their sins, and become, *"The voice of one crying in the wilderness: Prepare the way of the Lord, make his paths straight."*

John the Baptist starts a thriving career as a prophet baptizing people (pouring water over their heads to forgive sins) and preaching repentance. *"Repent, for the kingdom of heaven is at hand."*

John eventually baptizes Jesus one day and the heavens open up; the Holy Spirit of God descends like a dove and hovers over Jesus. God's voice rings out, "This is my beloved son, with whom I am well pleased." John looks at Jesus and says, *"Behold, the lamb of God, who takes away the sins of the world."*

John the Baptist ultimately gets arrested by the evil King Herod. At Herod's birthday party, the king promises a cute exotic dancer anything she wants and she says, *"Give me the head of John the Baptist here on a platter."* Herod agrees and delivers! Ay carumba. Sorry John.

The Devil Made Me Do It

Right after being baptized, the Holy Spirit leads Jesus into the wilderness. No locusts and honey for Jesus—he fasts for 40 days and 40 nights and afterward is super hungry. Enter the Devil, Satan, also called Beelzebub, the Prince of Demons, who slyly tempts Jesus. The Devil says, "If you're the son of God, command these stones to become loaves of bread," or perhaps a pepperoni pizza. Jesus responds with the famous quote, *"Man does not live by bread alone, but by every word that proceeds from the mouth of God."* Word up!

Jesus Takes the Stage

Jesus is now 30 years old and finally moves out of his parents' house and starts his mission. He travels the region performing awesome miracles and gaining notoriety. Among the miracles he performs, catalogued in the four Gospels, are: cooling fevers, casting out demons (exorcisms), forgiving sins, returning a dead girl to life, restoring sight to the blind, curing paralysis, managing leprosy, calming rough seas, rehabilitating a withered hand, fixing dumbness, and exorcizing a *legion of demons* from a possessed person then transferring the evil spirits into a herd of swine and drowning them. Woo hoo!

The 12 Apostles

During this traveling miracle show and preaching tour, Jesus recruits 12 special followers who will later spread the good news. These are the 12 Apostles, also called disciples. Their names are Peter, James, John, Andrew, Philip, Bartholomew, Matthew, Thomas, Thaddeus, Simon, Judas Iscariot, and another James.

The most famous is Peter, a fisherman on the Sea of Galilee. Jesus says to him, *"Follow me, and I will make you a fisher of men."* And later, *"You are Peter and upon this rock I will build my church."* Jesus promises him, *"The keys of the kingdom of heaven."* (Additional info not in Bible: After Jesus' death, Peter is said to have moved to Rome and become the first Pope of the Catholic Church, only to be crucified by the Romans. He's also depicted in folklore as manning the Gates of Heaven and handling admission, like a celestial bouncer.)

Jesus gives the Apostles the power to forgive sins, the ability to cast out demons, and cure every disease, and promises them outstanding telephone support, *"Whatever you ask in my name, I will do it . . . "*

(Additional info not in Bible: The Apostles later become saints, which are like demi-gods occupying an elevated position in heaven, just under the Holy Trinity composed of God, his son Jesus, and the Holy Spirit—three equal Gods in one. If you see a picture of the Vatican City square in Rome, the Apostles' statues are up on top of the outside columns.)

Another interesting note: There are some mentions in the Bible of siblings of Jesus, although these references are not clearly spelled out. His mother, the Virgin Mary, may have produced other children. One was named James, and there is disagreement among Christians about whether this James was one of the apostles named James. These kids may have been conceived the old-fashioned, nonimmaculate way.

Sermon on the Mount

Jesus brings his Apostles up on a mountain to teach them. The four Gospels give varying accounts, so here's a compilation of famous quotes: *"Love your enemies, do good to those who hate you, bless those who curse you, pray for those who abuse you." "If anyone strikes you on the right cheek, turn to him the other also . . . "* (Commonly referred to as: Turn the other cheek.) *"No city or house divided against itself will stand." "No one can serve two masters; for either he will hate the one and love the other, or he will be devoted to one and despise the other." "Judge not, that you be not judged." "Why do you see the speck that is in your brother's eye, but not notice the log that is in your own eye." "Ask, and it will be given to you; seek, and you will find; knock, and it will be opened to you."*

Jesus teaches them what later becomes known as The Lord's prayer: "*Our father who art in heaven, hallowed be thy name. Thy kingdom come. Thy will be done, on earth as it is in heaven. Give us this day our daily bread; and forgive us our debts, as we also have forgiven our debtors; And lead us not into temptation, but deliver us from evil.*" It's been reworked somewhat in the centuries that have followed.

Another group of sayings, the Beatitudes, also appear in the Semon on the Mount. "*Blessed are the poor in spirit, for theirs is the kingdom of heaven. Blessed are those who mourn, for they should be comforted. Blessed are the meek, for they shall inherit the earth. Blessed are those who hunger and thirst for righteousness, for they shall be satisfied. Blessed are the merciful, for they shall obtain mercy. Blessed are the pure in heart, for they shall see God. Blessed are the peacemakers, for they shall be called sons of God. Blessed are those who are persecuted for righteousness sake, for theirs is the kingdom of heaven. Blessed are you when men revile you and persecute you and utter all kinds of evil against you falsely on my account. Rejoice and be glad, for your reward is great in heaven, for so many persecuted the prophets who were before you.*"

These are all well-meaning, but there are also some real stinker quotes too. "Whoever marries a divorced woman commits adultery." "Everyone who looks at a woman lustfully has already committed adultery with her in his heart." "Do not give dogs what is holy; and do not throw your pearls before swine, lest they trample them underfoot, and turn to attack you." "Leave the dead to bury their own dead." "If your right hand causes you to sin, cut it off and throw it away; it is better that you lose one of your members then that your whole body be thrown into hell." (This may have spawned generations of lefties.)

New Commandment

An update to the Ten Commandments is provided by Jesus. This is commonly called the *Golden Rule*, but the Bible doesn't use that phrase.

Matthew's Gospel has Jesus teaching the Jewish priests (rabbis) when they ask him, "Teacher, which is the great commandment in the law?" And he replies, "You shall love the Lord your God with all your heart, and with all your soul, and with all your mind. This is the great and first commandment. And the second is like it, *You shall love your neighbor as yourself.* On these two commandments depend all the law and the prophets."

Multiplying Loaves and Fishes

Jesus is starting to attract large crowds to hear his preaching. Many scenes were like big outdoor concerts with Jesus speaking from a mountainside. One event lasted three days and the Apostles were trying to think of ways to feed all these people. "Jesus, we can't afford takeout for 5,000 people!" So Jesus told them to gather all the food they had—it was five or seven loaves of bread (depending on which Gospel you believe) and a few small fish. He told the crowd to sit, gave thanks, and then multiplied the loaves and fishes to feed everybody and even had more leftovers than he started with! "We're stuffed," groaned the happy crowd.

This act was so popular, Mark's Gospel has Jesus doing it at two events.

Separation of Church and State

Some of the very strict Jews, the Pharisees, asked Jesus, "Is it lawful to pay taxes to Caesar, or not?" (They may have been the very first tax attorneys.)

Jesus answers, "*Show me the money* for the tax." (Actual quote!) They give him a Roman coin. He points to Caesar's picture on the coin and says, "*Render therefore to Caesar the things that are Caesar's, and to God the things that are God's.*" When the Pharisees heard this, "they marveled; and went away." Possibly in search of a loophole.

Admission Requirements for Heaven

The heavenly afterlife is promised, but not for everyone. "*For many are called, but few are chosen.*" (There's always a "but.")

Jesus says, "*I am the way, I'm the truth, and the life; no one comes to the Father, but by me.*" "But many that are *first will be last, and the last first.*" "For this is the will of my Father, that everyone who sees the son and believes in him should have everlasting life; and I will raise him up upon the last day." "Go, sell all that you possess and give it to the poor, and you will have treasure in heaven; and come, follow me." "He who loves father or mother more than me is unworthy of me; and he who loves son or daughter more than me is not worthy of me; and he who does not take his cross and follow me is not worthy of me."

Only believers can be admitted to heaven. "He who believes in the son of God has eternal life; he who does not obey the son shall not see life, but the wrath of God rests upon him."

It's getting tougher—heaven is only open to believers who

are baptized. "Truly, truly, I say to you, unless one is born of water and the Spirit, he cannot enter the kingdom of God." "You must be born anew." Modern-day born-again Christians and many others take these passages literally.

Hold on, it's getting like a restricted country club. Only those who've participated in the ritual of communion (where bread and wine is turned into the body and blood of Jesus and eaten) can be admitted. "I say to you, unless you eat the flesh of the son of man and drink his blood, you have no life in you; he who eats my flesh and drinks my blood has eternal life, and I will raise him up at the last day."

Any place that doesn't welcome Jesus' disciples is targeted for a future drone strike. "Shake off the dust from your feet as you leave that town or house. Truly I say to you, it shall be more tolerable on the day of judgment for the land of Sodom and Gomorrah than for that town." You've been warned! *"With God all things are possible."*

Woe unto the Rich
Special disrespect is aimed at the wealthy rich folk, which remains an unresolved issue for modern-day churches and fat-cat believers. "Woe to you who are rich, for you have received your consolation." "How hard it will be for those who have riches to enter the kingdom of God?"

And the ever popular: *"It is easier for a camel to go through the eye of a needle than for a rich man to enter the kingdom of God."*

Walking on Water
Hmmm, things are getting heavy. So Jesus takes a break up in the woods on his own, and the Apostles go for a boat ride on the Sea of Galilee. Wouldn't you know it, night falls and a storm whips up the sea. The Apostles are miles from shore, rowing their boat as fast as they can and getting scared. Way after midnight in the rough waves, they see something slightly unusual. Somebody is actually out there walking on the water! At first they think it's a ghost, but when the person gets closer they realize it's that prankster Jesus! This is where the expression "WTF?" originated. Not to worry, Jesus says, "It is I; do not be afraid." They haul his butt into the boat and the seas calm down immediately. Matthew's Gospel version has Jesus inviting Peter out for a water stroll too!

Wedding at Cana
Jesus and his disciples score a wedding invitation in the town of Cana. Jesus' mother Mary is there too.

The reception party is rocking, but then the place runs out of wine. Mary tells Jesus, "Come on, do something." At first Jesus is just chilling, "Oh woman, what have you to do with me?" He doesn't like getting nagged, especially by his virgin mother, so he has the servants bring in six stone jars filled with water, and poof—turns them into even better wine than the party was serving before! Rock on partiers.

Casting Stones
One morning, Jesus goes over to the local temple near the Mount of Olives. A crowd is gathered because some drama is going down. The scribes and Pharisees have caught a woman

engaging in adultery! They ask Jesus to weigh in, reminding him that the Law of Moses calls for stoning until death by the whole town.

Jesus utters the famous quote, *"Let him who is without sin among you be the first to throw a stone* at her." The crowd shuffles around uncomfortably, hands in pockets, staring at the ground, then slowly disperses. Jesus tells her, "Go, and do not sin again."

The Pharisees and Jews in charge start to think about stoning Jesus instead.

Story of Lazarus
Lazarus is sometimes described as a leper, but in any case he's really sick. His relatives, who are friends of J. C., travel to find Jesus and ask for help. When they locate him, Jesus drops a bomb on them, "Sorry team, but Lazarus is already dead." Still, he agrees to go back with them to see what he can do.

When they arrive back in town, Lazarus has been dead and buried in a rock tomb for four days. Because the relatives are true believers, Jesus decides to prove he's really the son of God and yells, "Hey Lazarus, come out of there." And behold, Lazarus walks out of the tomb looking like a mummy. "Unbind him and let him go," says Jesus. Wow, it pays to have friends in high places.

This miracle is so over the top, it rattles the Jewish authorities even more.

Interesting note: horse-racing fans may remember track announcer Tom Durkin's famous line when Da Hoss came from way back in the pack to win the 1998 Breeders' Cup race: "This is the greatest comeback since Lazarus!"

Transfiguration

In case anyone is still not convinced of Jesus' divinity, here's a tale.

Jesus takes three of the Apostles up onto a very high mountain. "And he was transfigured before them, and his face shone like the sun, and his garments became white as light. And behold, there appeared to them Moses and Elijah, talking with Jesus . . . when lo, a bright cloud overshadowed them, and a voice from the cloud said, 'This is my beloved Son, with whom I am well pleased; listen to him.' When the disciples heard this, they fell on their faces, and were filled with awe. . . . And as they were coming down the mountain, Jesus commanded them, 'Tell no one the vision, until the Son of man is raised from the dead.'" Foreshadowing of the future.

The Great Judgment

The Gospels have some sections devoted to the end-of-the-world apocalypse. *The Last Judgment* is the title of Michelangelo's huge painting on the wall of the Vatican's Sistine Chapel in Rome.

Matthew's Gospel has the softest version of the apocalypse, with some famous quotes: "When the son of man comes in his glory, and all the angels with him, then he will sit on his glorious throne. Before him will be gathered all the nations, and he will separate them one from another as a shepherd separates the sheep from the goats, and he will place the sheep at his right hand, but the goats at the left. Then the King will say to those at his right hand, 'Come, O blessed of my Father, inherit the kingdom prepared for you from the foundation of the world; *for I was hungry and you gave me food, I was thirsty and you gave me drink, I was a stranger and you welcomed me, I was naked and you clothed me, I was sick and you visited me, I was in prison and you came to me.'"*

Then the good people scratch their heads and ask God, "When did we do that? And the King will answer them, 'Truly, I say to you, *as you did it to one of the least of these my brethren, you did it to me.'* Then he will say to those at his left hand, 'Depart from me, you cursed, into the eternal fire prepared for the devil and his angels.'" An everlasting world of hurt ensues.

The Prodigal Son

Jesus tells a parable about a man who had two sons and gave half his riches to each one. The younger one "took his journey to a far country, and there he squandered his property in loose living." When he spent it all, he bummed around some more, got a minimum wage job feeding swine, then returned home.

When the younger son comes back he says to his dad, "Father, I have sinned and am not worthy to even be a servant." Dad gives him a big hug, fancy robe, and throws an audacious party, *"he was lost, and is found."*

The older son hears the party going on and is mad because he's been working the fields since Junior took off. "You never gave me a party . . . but this other son has devoured your living with harlots!"

Dad replies, "Son, you are always with me . . . your brother was dead, and is alive."

The Good Samaritan

Robbers fell upon a traveler, stripped him, beat him, and left him half dead. A priest was going down the road and saw the victim, but kept right on going. A Samaritan came by next and stopped to help. He bandaged the victim's wounds, poured some wine, brought the poor guy to an inn, and paid the innkeeper to care for him. Jesus instructs, "Go and do likewise."

Jesus Stirs the Pot

It's not all warm fuzzy stories. There's some serious business to conduct.

"I came to cast fire upon the earth; and would that it were already kindled! . . . Do you think that I have come to give peace on earth? No, I tell you, but rather division . . . father against son and son against father . . . and daughter-in-law against mother-in-law . . . but unless you repent you will all likewise perish."

Hey now, ain't nobody got time for that! This was not welcome news. One crowd even tried to stone Jesus and he had to hide.

Welcome to Jerusalem

By now, Jesus' celebrity ranking (except for the occasional bad day as just mentioned) was in the stratosphere. The Jewish religious leaders in the capital of Jerusalem didn't like it one bit. He was stealing their marketshare and eating their lunch. The leaders were already holding a trump card they could play against him if needed: Jesus had performed miracles on the Sabbath, a major violation!

Now Jesus could have continued his great run in the suburbs, but he knew that if he was to be taken seriously as a messiah, he had to go to the big city to fulfill the Old Testament prophecies.

The Apostles knew this was dangerous and didn't want to go into Jerusalem. Jesus insisted and gave instructions to "get a young ass and colt." (True words to live by.) He then rode down the main road into the capital. People were waving palm-frond branches, welcoming Jesus as the messiah, King of Israel. "Behold, your king is coming, mounted on an ass." (Another true quote!) This event is still celebrated today by Christians as Palm Sunday.

Jesus loved to argue with the Pharisees and religious leaders. The city was getting ready for Passover and the priests were like, "We really don't need this now." One of Jesus' first stops was the Jewish Temple (which had been rebuilt after Solomon). Jesus comes in swinging! He enters the temple and sees a bunch of merchants—so he flies into a rage, overturns their tables, throws them all out including moneychangers and vendors selling pigeons! He yells, "My house shall be called a house of prayer; but you make it a den of robbers."

As if this commotion wasn't enough, he starts healing people right there! And he goes off on the leaders, "Woe to you scribes and Pharisees, hypocrites!" It's getting like reality TV, "you serpents, you brood of vipers, how are you to escape being sentenced to hell?" Whoa. At least he didn't F-bomb anybody (that we know of).

The Last Supper

Jesus knows he really blew the place up and the religious

leaders are going to get him. So later that week, he arranges a nice going-away dinner for his inner circle and Apostles, commonly called the Last Supper (still commemorated by Christians as Holy Thursday, just after Palm Sunday).

During dinner, Jesus predicts that one of the Apostles will betray him to the authorities. Jesus also predicts his own arrest, execution, and resurrection from the dead on the third day. This was not mere dinner chitchat.

Then Jesus gives them the *communion ritual* still practiced today as Mass. It's only a few sentences in three of the four Gospels (curiously, there's no Last Supper in John); nonetheless, this ritual is the major exercise and focal point in many Christian denominations.

Matthew's version is: "Now as they were eating, Jesus took bread, and blessed, and broke it, and gave it to the disciples and said, *'Take, eat; this is my body.'* And he took a cup, and when he had given thanks he gave it to them, saying, *'Drink of it, all of you; for this is my blood* of the covenant, which is poured out for many for the forgiveness of sins.'"

This is what's occurring when believers line up and are given a bread wafer and sometimes a sip of wine, known as holy communion.

Judas

Sure enough, the betrayal prediction comes true. The Apostle named Judas Iscariot accepts a bribe of silver from the chief priests and elders to identify Jesus. He comes up with a secret signal, *"The one I shall kiss is the man; seize him."*

That's why the name Judas is synonymous with traitor and a Judas kiss is not a good thing.

Pontius Pilate

Jesus is seized and arrested by the Jews and dragged before the Roman governor, Pontius Pilate. Pilate's like, "What's he done? There's no crime here." But the Jewish clergy persists: He's blasphemous, says he's the King of the Jews, did a healing on the Sabbath, riles up the people, and he doesn't even scoop up after his dog (wait, not that last one).

Pilate rolls his eyes, but wants to keep the high priests happy and avoid a riot. So he says, "Well, Passover's almost here and it's traditional to release one prisoner. Should I release Jesus Christ, the King of the Jews and messiah; or Barabbas, this stinking, no good, convicted murderer."

Pilate's shocked when the crowd yells to release Barabbas! "Are you sure? What should I do with the King of the Jews?" And the mob screams, *"Crucify him!"* Pilate says, "Well, okay."

Crucifixion

Warning: things are about to get gruesome. Reader discretion advised.

So the next day (still commemorated by Christians as Good Friday), Jesus is mocked and tortured. He carries his own wooden cross uphill, is nailed to it, and is speared in the side. A crown of thorns also gets put on his head along with a sign saying King of the Jews.

The cross is stood up in the ground, alongside two convicted thieves on their crosses. That's why you sometimes see three crosses set up outside churches.

After nine hours, Jesus utters his last words, *"My God, my God, why has thou forsaken me?"* Then dies. The earth turns dark and the curtain of the temple in Jerusalem is torn in two.

Later, Joseph of Arimethea carries his body to a cave tomb and rolls a large rock across the entrance.

The Resurrection

On Sunday, today celebrated by Christians as Easter, some women followers (including one named Mary Magdalene) go to the cave and see the rock has been rolled aside. Gospel accounts vary, but they then see one or two (or none) young men in white robes (angels), who tell them, *"He is not here, he has risen."*

Post-Resurrection Appearances

For the next few weeks, the risen Jesus appears to many followers to prove that he did indeed rise from the dead and is the son of God.

Again, the four Gospel stories vary widely, but he appears to the now 11 Apostles (Judas was kicked out), Mary Magdalene, and other people we don't know.

The Apostles are stressed and desperately need a vacation, so they head to the Sea of Tiberias, which is nice that time of year. Peter says, "I am going fishing." And who can blame him? The others chime in, "We will go with you."

They're in their boat at dawn, not catching anything, when who do they see standing on the beach? Jesus Christ himself! He even tells the Apostles where to drop their nets to haul in a big school of fish. Then, miraculously, Jesus invites them to breakfast and cooks some of the fish and bread. I am not making this up.

Doubting Thomas

John's Gospel is the only one that contains this next semi-famous story. Another time, Jesus appeared to all the remaining Apostles as a group, except Thomas, who was busy that day (maybe with a fake dental appointment).

The other disciples tell Thomas about Jesus' appearance and he doesn't believe them. Thomas says, "Unless I see him, and put my fingers in the holes where they nailed him on the cross, I won't believe it."

Eight days later, Jesus appears to doubting Thomas and let's him touch his wounds. No-longer-doubting Thomas proclaims, "My Lord and my God!"

Ascension

Jesus appears to the Apostles yet again. He tells them to go out and preach the good news to mankind. "He who believes and is baptized will be saved; but he who does not believe is condemned." (I wouldn't call that purely good news.)

Jesus then is miraculously lifted up into the air and actually ascends all the way to heaven and sits down at the right hand of God. This occurence is still celebrated as the Feast of the Ascension.

John 3:16

Before we leave the Gospels, you may have noticed that there always seems to be some guy at sporting events, such as in the end-zone seats of every football game ever played, holding up a sign that says, John 3:16. What the hell is this?

It refers to the Gospel of John, chapter 3, verse 16, which reads, "*For God so loved the world that he gave his only son, that whoever believes in him should not perish but have eternal life. Now back to our halftime show."* (Sorry, not that last part.)

23

Acts of the Apostles

This book tells how the Apostles started to spread the good news and begin the early Christian church.

But first, some loose ends to tie up. Judas Iscariot, the traitor, reportedly used his silver bribe money to buy a field. But while on the field he fell down, "burst open his middle, and all his bowels gushed out." Hah! Justice is served.

Next, the Apostles choose a replacement for Judas to bring the number back up to 12. They narrow it down to two candidates, then "cast lots," which is throwing dice, and choose Matthias. So much for divine inspiration.

The 12 are gathered together on the Jewish feast of Pentecost (when the Law was given), and *a mighty wind from heaven* fills their house. Tongues of fire appear and rest on each one of them. They're filled with the Holy Spirit and start to *speak in tongues*. The chapter uses this magical story to explain how the Apostles were able to preach in different languages. Taking a cue from this story, modern-day Pentecostal Christians regularly scream out gibberish when they're filled with the

Holy Spirit and claim they're *speaking in tongues*. Miracle or lunacy, you decide.

Those who heard the Apostles speak in tongues were "amazed and perplexed. But others mockingly said, 'They are filled with new wine.'" Peter has to stand up and bail them out, "For these men are not drunk, as you suppose, since it is only the third hour of the day." (Well played! Obviously no one drinks that early!) I guess Peter convinced most observers.

Okay now, enough messing around, you boys get to work. The Apostles start to preach repentance, forgive sins, and baptize new converts. Their first day they add 3,000 followers!

They also start to heal all sorts of maladies and cast out demons from the possessed, and Peter even restores life to a dead girl named Tabitha.

Word is spreading and enrollment is soaring. Believers are selling everything they have and giving the money to the Apostles (who then distribute it). They even convert a Roman centurion. Bravo!

The Jewish religious authorities are jealous and extremely mad. They arrest the Apostles and jail them. But hark, that night an angel of the Lord opens the prison doors and leads them out.

Not to be deterred, the Jews and Pharisees lock them up again. But Peter gives an eloquent speech and the Pharisees are afraid of a rebellious melee—so they just beat the Apostles and tell them to stop preaching. "Knock it off and get lost."

Thus begins a back and forth power struggle. The Apostles won't quit and the Jews strike back. James and a new preacher, Stephen, are killed, making them early martyrs of the Christian church. Peter is imprisoned and put in chains. Another angel has to appear, undo the cuffs, use telepathy to have a massive iron gate "open of its own accord," and sneak Peter out.

Some of the Apostles break into smaller groups and start traveling and preaching to other areas around Israel. The persecution continues.

Saul of Tarsus

Saul was one of the Jews who was bullying the Apostles and new Christians around. He was also a "person of interest" in the stoning death of Stephen. One day Saul was on the road to Damascus, when suddenly a bright light from heaven blinded him and knocked him to the ground. The voice of Jesus rang out, "Saul, Saul, why do you persecute me?" Saul gets up and fumbles his way into town. After three days of blindness, God sends a Christian to Saul. God's plan is to recruit Saul and have him convert all the Gentiles (non-Jews). The Christian messenger cures his blindness, and Saul becomes an enthusiastic Christian convert, is baptized, and changes his name to Paul.

Paul (later St. Paul) is filled with the Holy Spirit, learns from the Apostles, and then sets out with different helpers to Cyprus, Greece, and Asia Minor. He becomes a gifted speaker and prolific letter writer, and converts many people to Christianity.

It's not always easy. Along the way he is stoned and dragged out of one city, beaten with rods, and arrested and thrown in prison multiple times. On one occasion God sends a "great earthquake" to open the prison doors and spring him. In Athens, Paul debates the Stoic philosophers who diss him to his face with, "What is this babbler saying?" (True story.)

Paul has the power to perform miracles, mostly the usual healing and exorcism types. One amusing story does occur. Paul is somewhere in Greece and is giving a long-winded talk that goes on well past midnight. A young man, Eutychus, is sitting by a third-floor window listening and falls asleep. Eutychus falls out the window, hits the ground, and dies. Paul runs down and brings him back to life. Ta-dah, close call. (Perfect time to add a new Bible verse: "Blessed are the brief." But no, a missed opportunity.)

Paul heads back to Jerusalem and has another rough go of it. He's preaching in a temple when he gets dragged outside and the Jews almost kill him. Roman soldiers stop the mob and take Paul into protective custody. The Romans aren't sure what to do with him so they call in the chief Jewish priests to have a big tribunal at the Sanhedrin. Paul gets to tell his story to a larger audience (which he loves doing).

The Jews plot to kill him, so the Roman governor bounces him to another province where Paul again gives a grand oration in the courtroom. The Acts of the Apostles is turning into the All About Paul Show.

This goes on again and finally the local King Agrippa says, "Let's put him on a boat to Italy and they can try him there." The entire audience agrees.

Paul is quickly deposited on the next boat out. The ship sails the Mediterranean and passes the island of Cyprus. Ever the drama queen, Paul starts telling everybody on board that the voyage is doomed and they should get on land, like right now.

Soon a tempest blows in and the crew has to throw cargo over to avoid sinking. Paul says, "I told you so. But don't worry, an angel informed me we'll survive, but he did mention something about running aground."

They weather the storm, but 14 days later the boat hits a shoal and the bow gets firmly stuck. The ship's stern is then broken up by the waves. The captain tells everyone, "You're all free, abandon ship and swim for shore." Everyone washes up on the island of Malta.

Paul makes friends with the natives by healing the chief's father and other islanders. Three months later they get a new boat and successfully sail to Italy. Once there, Paul bunks in with other Christians. He finally makes his way to the capital city of Rome, as a free man.

Once in Rome, Paul attempts to convert the local Italian Jews, but strikes out again. So he shifts back to what he does best, preaching and converting the Gentiles.

24

The Letter of Paul to the Romans

Even though Paul wasn't a big hit in Rome, it didn't stop him from writing a long-winded letter to the early Christians there. It's basically Paul's personal spin on all the history and teachings we've heard earlier.

There are a couple notable quotes: "*For the wages of sin is death,* but the free gift of God is eternal life in Christ Jesus our Lord." And, "O the depths of the riches and wisdom and knowledge of God! *How unsearchable are his judgments and how inscrutable his ways!*" Usually paraphrased as: *"How inscrutable are God's ways."* A line still used today to "explain" bad events.

25

The First Letter of Paul
to the Corinthians

This is a letter to the early Christian community of Corinth in the Roman province of Achaia. Paul elaborates on teachings and tries to settle internal disputes that have apparently arisen. "For in the first place; when you assemble as a church, I hear that there are divisions among you."

The first dispute involves the dress code. So Paul gives some guidance: "For if a woman will not veil herself, then she should cut off her hair; but if it is disgraceful for a woman to be shorn or shaven, let her wear a veil. For a man ought not to cover his head since he is the image and glory of God." Another dispute involves the place of women. Paul smooths that out too: "As in all the churches of the saints, the women should keep silence in the churches. For they are not permitted to speak, but should be subordinate, as even the law says. If there is anything they desire to know, let them ask their husbands at home. For it is shameful for a woman to speak in church."

Some famous quotes are offered. "Do you not know that *your body is a temple* of the Holy Spirit within you, which you have from God?" Usually shortened to, "Treat your body as a temple."

"*And if I have all faith, so as to remove mountains,* but have not love, I am nothing." Spin-doctored loosely to "Faith can move mountains."

And a favorite at weddings: "*Love is patient and kind; love is not jealous or boastful; it is not arrogant or rude. Love does not insist on its own way; it is not irritable or resentful; it does not rejoice at wrong, but rejoices in the right. Love bears all things, believes all things, hopes all things, endures all things.*"

Paul ends this letter with some instruction on the touchy subject of contributions. "Now concerning the contribution for the saints: so you also are to do. On the first day of every week, each of you is to put something aside and store it up, as he may prosper, so that contributions need not be made when I come. And when I arrive, I will send those whom you accredit by letter to carry your gift to Jerusalem. If it seems advisable that I should go also, they will accompany me." In other words, start saving up regularly because I'll be picking up the loot when I arrive.

26

The Second Letter
of Paul to the Corinthians

It appears that some vague drama went down when Paul went to Corinth to pick up the contributions. The second letter is sort of an apology for another missing letter, probably the world's first nasty-gram. "For I wrote you out of much affliction and anguish of heart and with many tears. . . . For I made up my mind not to make you another painful visit." Sounds like he should not have hit send.

What was the drama about that turned the visit painful? Some hints are given. Maybe diverting funds, "Some suspect us of acting in worldly fashion." Maybe some questionable quotes or pronouncements, "Since you desire proof that Christ is speaking in me."

Maybe other traveling preachers are swaying the flock, "I feel a divine jealousy for you, for I betrothed you to Christ. . . . But I am afraid that as the serpent deceived Eve by his cunning, your thoughts will be led astray. . . . For such men are false apostles, deceitful workmen, disguising themselves as apostles of Christ."

Paul does a lot of tap dancing to quiet things down and reminds the congregation, "Any charge must be sustained by the evidence of two or three witnesses." So there, no one saw me do nothin'.

Remarkably, Paul takes another run at fundraising for his next visit! "You will be enriched in every way for your great generosity, which through us will produce thanksgiving to God; for the rendering of the service not only supplies the wants of the saints but also overflows in many thanksgivings to God. Under the test of this service, you will glorify God by your obedience in acknowledging the gospel of Christ, and by the generosity of your contribution for them and for all others; while they long for you and pray for you, because of the surpassing grace of God in you. Thanks be to God for his inexpressible gift!" Don't forget to give generously.

27

The Letter of Paul
to the Galatians

Now Paul has a real fire to put out. The churches he started in Asia Minor are being infiltrated by Jewish preachers telling them they have to become Jews first before Christians! Dang Hebrews again.

First, Paul spreads a little guilt. "I am astonished that you are so quickly deserting him who called you in the grace of Christ and turning to a different gospel—not that there is another gospel, but there are some who trouble you and want to pervert the gospel of Christ."

And for those pervert preachers, how about a curse. "If anyone is preaching to you a gospel contrary to that which you received, let him be accursed." You go Rev!

Remember people, I'm the one who converts the Gentiles and Peter does the Jews. "I have been entrusted with the gospel to the uncircumcised, just as Peter has been entrusted with the gospel to the circumcised." So check your wieners and get back in line. Paul settles the issue by telling the Gentiles that you don't have to be a Jew and a Christian. The Jews are old news. Once Jesus Christ arrived, there's a new sheriff in town. "So that the [old Jewish] law was our custodian until Christ came, that we might be justified by faith. But now that faith has come, we are no longer under a custodian."

28

The Letter of Paul to the Ephesians

Paul had plenty of time to write this letter since he was in jail. So he fills the Ephesians in on some teachings. Ephesus was a town in what's now the country of Turkey.

First up, women again: "As the church is subject to Christ, so let wives be subject in everything to their husbands."

Next, a clarification on slavery: "Slaves, be obedient to those who are your earthly masters, with fear and trembling, in singleness of heart, as to Christ." Paul does throw them a bone though, a glimmer of hope for the next life: "Knowing that whatever good anyone does, he will receive the same again from the Lord, whether he is a slave or free." So there's some reward slaves can look forward to.

Then Paul serves up a religious military analogy. "Therefore take the whole *armor of God*, that you may be able to withstand in the evil day, and having done all, to stand. Stand therefore, having *girded your loins with truth*, and having put on *the breastplate of righteousness*, and having shod your feet with the equipment of the gospel of peace; besides all these, taking the *shield of faith*, with which you can quench all the flaming darts of the evil one. And take the *helmet of salvation*, and the *sword of the Spirit*, which is the word of God." This will come in handy during holy wars and crusades.

29

The Letter of Paul
to the Philippians

Paul's still in jail. The Philippians are in Macedonia, a region of Greece. Wassup P-dogs? Same old, same old, nothing new to report.

30

The Letter of Paul
to the Colossians

Trouble is brewing in the podunk town of Colossae in Asia Minor. Paul sends a letter from, where else, jail.

The Colossians are shifting to false teachers, practicing self-abasement, fasting, and worshipping angels! Paul points out the error of their ways.

31

The First and Second
Letters of Paul
to the Thessalonians

We'll lump these two letters together. Thessalonica is the capital city of the Macedonian region of Greece.

Paul starts by kissing up to the Thessalonians, telling them what good believers they are and thanking them for how well they treated Paul and his helpers on their recent visit. Which was a welcome relief, we now learn, after those jackasses at Philippi "shamefully treated" Paul and his crew and ran them out of town!

The Thessalonians know better and will receive salvation when God and Jesus return and smite the nonbelievers. "When the Lord Jesus is revealed from heaven with his mighty angels and flaming fire, inflicting vengeance upon those who do not know God and upon those who do not obey the gospel of our Lord Jesus. They shall suffer the punishment of eternal destruction and exclusion from the presence of the Lord and from the glory of his might, when he comes on that day to be glorified in his saints, and to be marveled at all who have believed, because our testimony to you was believed."

The Thessalonians are cool with that, but want to know when Jesus is coming back to earth, like next week or this summer or Tuesday? So Paul crafts a slick answer for them in his letter. "For you yourselves know well that *the day of the Lord will come like a thief in the night.* When people say, 'There is peace and security,' then sudden destruction will come upon them. . . . But you are not in darkness, brethren, for that day to surprise you like a thief." (Unlike those nonbelievers who will be totally stunned.) So remember, you've got that ace in the hole.

Oh yeah, one more thing. It has come to Paul's attention that some Thessalonians are getting lazy and not pulling their own weight around church. Time for a rebuke: "Keep away from any brother living in idleness. . . . We gave you this command: *If anyone will not work, let him not eat.* For we hear that some of you are living in idleness, mere busybodies, not doing any work." What do you think this is, a charity operation?

32

The First and Second
Letters of Paul to Timothy

The All About Paul Show is winding down and Paul is getting ready for retirement. He gives his opinions and practical advice to one of his successors, Timothy.

But first he does a little gossiping of his own about some bad preachers—and he names names! "By rejecting conscience, certain persons have *made shipwreck of their faith,* among them Hymenae'us and Alexander, whom I have delivered to Satan that they may learn not to blaspheme." Harsh!

Now some tips on how to run the church. On women: "I permit no woman to teach or to have authority over men; she has to keep silent. For Adam was formed first, then Eve; Adam was not deceived, but the woman was deceived and became a transgressor." We've heard that before.

On how to select bishops: "Now a bishop must be above all reproach, the husband of one wife, temperate . . . no drunkard, not violent, and no lover of money. . . . He must not be a recent convert, or he may be puffed up with conceit and fall into the condemnation of the devil."

On deacons: "Deacons likewise must be serious, not double-tongued, not addicted to much wine, not greedy for gain."

Regarding money, there are some famous quotes. *"For we brought nothing into the world, and we cannot take anything out of the world. . . . For the love of money is the root of all evil . . . fight the good fight of faith."*

33

The Letter of Paul to Titus

Titus is another of Paul's helpers who will be carrying on the mission. Paul must know that Titus will be competing against those pesky Jewish preachers, so he gives him a pep talk about them. Even going so far as to label them the Circumcision Party, like the Tea Party!

"For there are many insubordinate men, empty talkers and deceivers, especially the circumcision party; they must be silenced, since they are upsetting whole families by teaching for base gain what they have no right to teach.... Instead of giving heed to Jewish myths or to commands of men who reject the truth ... They profess to know God, but they denied him by their deeds; they are detestable, disobedient, unfit for any good deed." Yo, Paul, tell us how you really feel.

But anyway Titus, just try to "avoid stupid controversies, genealogies, dissensions, and quarrels over the law, for they are unprofitable and futile." Good luck my man.

34

The Letter of Paul
to Philemon

This looks like Paul's last letter. He is now in jail in Rome and the end is near. But a tricky little problem crops up in prison that needs some fast but tactful letter writing.

Philemon is a fat-cat believer in the congregation Paul started in Colossae. It seems that one of Philemon's slaves ran away and stole some stuff on his way out.

Well, the slave, Onesimus, ends up in the same jail as Paul in Rome, and Paul converts and befriends him! Now what to do? Say slavery is wrong and risk ticking off the big donor, master Philemon? Or keep Onesimus as Paul's own jailhouse slave? Or send him back?

Paul, ever the diplomat, starts schmoozing Philemon. "I have derived much joy and comfort from your love, my brother. . . . Accordingly, although I am bold enough in Christ to command you to do what is required, yet for love's sake I prefer to appeal to you. . . . I appeal to you for my child,

Onesimus, whose father I have become in my imprisonment."

So far, so good. Paul has a shot at the Emancipation Proclamation nearly two millennia early, but drops the ball, "I am sending him back to you, I would have been glad to keep him with me, in order that he might serve me on your behalf during my imprisonment for the gospel. . . . Perhaps this is why he was parted from you for a while, that you might have him back forever." Near miss, almost an end to slavery!

Additional FYI—some recent authorities have written that St. Paul may have been a repressed gay man himself. Gives an additional level of meaning to this story. Who knew?!

35

The Letter to the Hebrews

Written by an anonymous author, this letter is to a group of Jewish converts to Christianity who are considering going back to Judaism. The converts are reminded that Jesus Christ is above all the Old Testament prophets, angels, Moses, and Joshua because he was the son of God. See? Now it's clear. They're further reminded that they can be saved only if they remain converted Christians. "*Today, when you hear his voice, do not harden your hearts.*"

The second sales pitch tells the wavering converts they'd be wasting their time going back to Judaism. They'd be living in the past and offering sacrifices with the blood of goats and bulls. Jesus brought the new covenant and sealed it with his own blood so that we could have forgiveness of sins. It essentially says, "So come on, get with the modern program and embrace the new faith. Noah, Abraham, Moses, and the old Jewish characters had strong faith, why don't you?"

Other verbose and equally persuasive arguments for remaining Christian are offered.

36

The Letter of James and First and Second Letters of Peter

These letters can be grouped together. They offer encouragement and reminders to the early Christians. Among the items: Be holy, love one another, you are God's people, respect the local rulers and Emperor of Rome, endure persecution—you'll be blessed since you're sharing Jesus' suffering—be sober, watch out for the Devil, and beware of greedy false prophets.

37

First, Second, and Third Letters of John and the Letter of Jude

These letters represent a grab bag of ideas. We hear the first mention of the term "antichrist." A dude name Diotropes does not acknowledge John's authority and has been bad mouthing him, "prating against me with evil words."

We have one notable quote: *"God is love, and he who abides in love abides in God, and God abides in him."*

There's obviously a recurring problem with false preachers. Anyone who doesn't teach that Jesus was the son of God is labeled as false. Jude's letter goes further, calling such preachers out as "grumblers, malcontents, following their own passions, loudmouth boasters, flattering people to gain advantage." Picky, picky.

But don't worry folks, 'cause a holy judgment is a comin'.

38

Book of Revelation

Brace yourselves people of planet Earth. The grand finale is here: Revelation of Jesus, Apocalypse, Armageddon, Great Judgment, Destruction, Second Coming, Good versus Evil, Angels versus Demons, Jesus versus Satan in an Ultimate Cage Match, End Times, Rapture, Tribulations, Numerology, Plagues, Beasts, Whores, Wrath, Trumpets, Fire, and more Ass Kicking Than Ever Seen Before—all in 3-D Technicolor IMAX Surround Sound! You don't want to miss this! We'll go through it in detail because so many movies, shows, and books about mystery, horror, the occult, the paranormal, unexplained phenomena, and prophecy invariably have references that come right from here.

But first, the Book of Revelation begins with a message to each of the seven early Christian churches, in seven obscure towns, including Philadelphia. (True, the churches named are Ephesus, Smyrna, Pergamum, Thyatica, Sardis, Philadelphia, and Laodicea.) The letters to the churches start out nice enough, "Grace to you and peace from *him who is and who was and is to come.* . . . . I know you are enduring patiently and bearing up for my name's sake." Then each church is given a, "But I have this against you . . ." enumerating specific ways they are not performing adequately. Missteps like listening to false Jewish prophets (especially the prophetess Jezebel!), eating food sacrificed to idols, and fraternizing with the "synagogue of Satan." Pretty standard stuff. Something tells me all the early Christian converts were getting antsy and tired of waiting around for the Second Coming. They may have been like: "Jesus, why aren't you back here yet, you promised, let's go already." So the author leads them on: "Hey, seven churches, straighten up and '*Repent, for the time is near.*'"

These introductory messages and the Book of Revelation were written by John. It's not clear if it's the same John who wrote the fourth Gospel. Even way back then, it was a common name. This John explains he was exiled to the rocky island of Patmos by the Roman Emperor for preaching the Christian good news. I'd be willing to bet that John found some hallucinogenic plants or mushrooms growing on rocky Patmos. See for yourselves.

While enjoying his exile, John heard a "loud voice like a trumpet" behind him saying, "Write what you see in a book and send it to the seven churches." He turns to look for the voice and sees "Seven golden lampstands, and in the midst of the lampstands one like a son of man, clothed with a long robe and with a golden girdle round his breast; his head and his hair were white as white wool, white as snow; his eyes were like a flame of fire, his feet were like burnished bronze. . . . In his right hand he held seven stars, from his mouth issued a sharp two edge sword, and his face was like the sun shining in full strength." John falls down on the ground and the image says, "*I am the first and the last. . . . I am the Alpha and the Omega.*" This is relatively tame compared with what comes next.

John looks up and a door to heaven opens. A voice beckons him to "Come up hither, and I will show you what must take place after this." John is transported into heaven and sees a great throne surrounded by a rainbow and 24 other thrones "where sit elders dressed in white garments and gold crowns." Cue the "flashes of lightning, voices, peals of thunder, seven torches of fire, and a sea of glass like crystal."

Wait, there's more. "On each side of the throne, are four living creatures, full of eyes in front and behind: the first living creature like a lion, the second living creature like an ox, the third living creature with the face of a man, and the fourth living creature like a flying eagle. And the four living creatures, each of them with six wings, are full of eyes all around and within, and day and night they never cease to sing."

"And I saw in the right hand of him who was seated on the throne a scroll written within and on the back, *sealed with seven seals*; and I saw a strong angel proclaiming with a loud voice, 'Who is worthy to open the scroll and break its seals?' And no one in heaven or on earth or under the earth was able to open the scroll."

"And between the throne and the four living creatures and among the elders, I saw a Lamb standing, as though it had been slain, with seven horns and with seven eyes, which are the seven spirits of God sent out into all the earth; and he went and took the scroll from the right hand of him who was seated on the throne. And when he had taken the scroll, the four living creatures and the 24 elders fell down before the Lamb, each holding a harp, and with golden bowls full of incense, which are the prayers of the saints; and they sang a new song, saying, 'Worthy art thou to take the scroll and to open its seals, for thou wast slain and by thy blood did ransom men for God.'" (Note: the Lamb is generally interpreted as representing Jesus Christ.)

Seven Seals and Four Horsemen

Next, the Lamb opens the *seven seals* one by one. Each of the first four seals release a different color horse and rider who gallop down to earth.

The *first horse is white* and its rider has a crown and an archery bow. This symbolizes a *conquering power*. Next, *a red horse and rider with a "great sword," unleashes war* on the earth.

The third seal is opened, "And behold, *a black horse,* and its rider had a balance in his hand" representing *famine which follows war.*

When the Lamb opens the fourth seal, "Behold, *a pale horse, and its rider's name was Death, and Hades followed him*; and they were given power over a fourth of the earth, to kill with sword and with famine and with pestilence and by wild beasts of the earth." Although the Bible doesn't use the specific title, the Four Horsemen of the Apocalypse, they are known as Conquest, War, Famine, and Death.

As if that wasn't bad enough, we've still got three seals to break on the scroll! The fifth seal opens up an area under a heavenly altar, holding all the souls that were recently martyred for Jesus. They cry out, "Lord, how long until you have avenged our blood?" Each is given a white robe and told to standby.

"When he opened the sixth seal, I looked, and behold, there was a great earthquake; and the sun became black as sackcloth, the full moon became like blood, and the stars in the sky fell to the earth as the fig tree sheds its winter fruit when shaken by gale; the sky vanished like a scroll that is rolled up, and every mountain and island was removed from its place."

Before the seventh and final seal is opened, it's time for some housekeeping. John sees four angels standing at the four corners of the earth (because the earth is flat), and a fifth angel rises from the sun with the last seal and instructs the other four, "Do not harm the earth or the sea or the trees, till we have sealed the servants of our God on their foreheads."

John explains that a special forehead insignia will be used to identify the good guys—144,000 men total, 12,000 from each of the 12 tribes of Israel, are marked on the forehead. This proves that plenty of Jews, the original chosen people, will have converted to worship the Lamb (Jesus), and are thus eligible to be saved.

Now back to live action! The Lamb breaks open the seventh seal and there is silence for half an hour. (Pause for dramatic effect, the suspense is building!) Seven angels stand before God, they received seven trumpets and an incense holder. One angel puts fire from God's altar into the incense holder. He takes a practice swing, winds up, and flings that bucket straight down toward earth! Once more, cue the "peals of thunder, voices, flashes of lightning, and an earthquake."

Get ready audience, "Now the seven angels who had the seven trumpets made ready to blow them. The first angel blew his trumpet, and there followed hail and fire, mixed with blood, which fell on the earth; and a third of the earth was burnt up, and a third of the trees were burnt up, and all green grass was burnt up."

"The second angel blew his trumpet, and something like a great mountain, burning with fire, was thrown into the sea; and a third of the sea became blood, a third of the living creatures in the sea died, and a third of the ships were destroyed. The third angel blew his trumpet, and a great star fell from heaven, blazing like a torch, and it fell on a third of the rivers and on the fountains of water." The fourth angel blows, and one third of the sun, moon, and stars go dark.

By this time, a third of the audience has crawled under their surround sound theater seats! So, to avoid a mass nervous breakdown, we get a slight respite. "An eagle crying with a loud voice, as it flew in midheaven, '*Woe, woe, woe to those who dwell on the earth,* at the blasts of the other trumpets which the three angels are about to blow!'"

The fifth angel blows and a single star falls from heaven to earth, opening a bottomless pit with smoke coming out. Hark, that wasn't so bad; I was expecting worse. Well not so fast, this is the first of *three woes* predicted by the eagle. Up from the smoking pit fly swarms of locusts! These are not your ordinary pests; oh no, they are given the power to "sting men like scorpions." But they only sting the non-converted humans who don't have the special seal of God stamped on their foreheads. These locusts also look a little different than usual, they "were like horses arrayed for battle; on their heads were what looked like crowns of gold; their faces were like human faces, their hair like womens' hair, and their teeth like lions' teeth; they had scales like iron breastplates, and the noise of their wings was like the noise of many chariots with horses rushing into battle. They have tails like scorpions." These varmints embark across the earth on a five month stinging spree, gang-stanging the non-believers! So ends the first woe, two to go.

Enter angel number six with his trumpet. He releases "the four angels who are bound by the great river Euphrates." These four scoundrels lead thousands of cavalry soldiers who massacre another third of mankind. Not so horrible you say— well the horses had heads of lions and "sulphur issued from their mouths." Oh and by the way, they had serpent tails with snakeheads on the ends that bite too. Ouchy.

Two woes down and the remaining miserable inhabitants of the planet still won't repent; they insist on worshipping demons and idols, stealing, and tolerating sorcerers. Some people never learn.

Okay, the last angel with a trumpet is a "mighty angel coming down from heaven, wrapped in a cloud, with a rainbow over his head, and his face was like the sun, and his legs like pillars of fire. He had a little scroll open in his hand." A voice from heaven says to John, "Do not write this down." Just take the little scroll from the angel and eat it, because it's a secret. Holy Mother of God—what a cheesy theatrical trick! You can't leave us hanging like this!

John is then given a tape measure and sent to take some boring measurements of the temple. I guess the one in Jerusalem but it's not spelled out. He's also given two witnesses, clothed in sackcloth, who can issue prophecies for the next 1,260 days. Apocalypse interruptus.

This acid trip movie is getting monumentally weird. Perhaps John's drug level is hitting a trough. We just might have to wait for the sequel. I can't take it!

Intermission ensues. John must've found some more magic mushrooms to ingest, and the Book of Revelation's destruction of the universe mercifully continues.

The seventh angel reappears and finally blows his trumpet. As you recall, we've still got another woe to go! Loud voices in heaven proclaim, "The kingdom of the world has become the kingdom of our Lord and of his Christ, and he shall reign forever and ever." Okay good, it was just a momentary lapse.

More flashes of lightning, voices, peals of thunder, an earthquake, and now even "heavy hail" begins to rain down. (Probably baseball sized.) Against this backdrop, "two portents appear." The first is, "A woman clothed with the sun, with the moon under her feet, and on her head a crown of 12 stars; she was with child and she cried out in her pangs of birth, in anguish for delivery."

The second portent then appears, "Behold, a great red dragon, with seven heads and 10 horns, and seven diadems (jeweled crowns) upon his head. His tail swept down a third of the stars of heaven, and cast them to the earth. And the dragon stood before the woman who was about to bear a child, that he might devour her child when she brought it forth; she brought forth a male child, one who is to rule all the nations with a rod of iron, but her child was caught up to God and to his throne." Delivered, snatched, and rescued in the nick of time!

Ready to rumble. "Now war arose in heaven, Michael and his angels fighting against the dragon; and the dragon and his angels fought, but they were defeated and there was no longer any place for them in heaven. And the great dragon was thrown down, that ancient serpent, who was called the Devil and Satan, the deceiver of the whole world—he was thrown down to the earth, and his angels were thrown down with him." The Devil dragon chases the woman around earth, but she sprouts two eagle wings to fly away and escape. So the dragon wages war on the remaining believers on earth.

Sea Beast

The Devil dragon gives power to a nautical beast. "And I saw *a beast rising out of the sea,* with 10 horns and seven heads, 10 diadems upon its horns and a blasphemous name written upon its heads. And the beast that I saw was like a leopard, its feet were like a bear's, and its mouth was like a lion's mouth." And just to be even more frightening, the beast has a potty mouth! "And the beast was given a mouth uttering haughty and blasphemous words," and the sea beast ruled the earth for 42 months, cussing up a storm no doubt.

Wouldn't you know, the surviving humans, who don't have God's special forehead stamp, start to worship the sea beast! It's true: You just can't fix stupid.

One notable quote: " ... *if anyone slays with the sword, with the sword he must be slain.*" Commonly translated as *"Live by the sword, die by the sword."*

The Land Beast and the Mark of the Devil

"Then I saw *another beast which rose out of the earth;* it had two horns like a lamb and it spoke like a dragon."

The land beast can perform some fire tricks, but its main mission is to deceive men into building an idol of the sea beast. Another graven image! Then the land beast breathes into the idol and it starts talking, urging the dumb humans to worship it more and slaying anyone who doesn't.

The land beast has another special power: the ability to *mark men on the forehead or right-hand with the "number of the beast's name."* His special number is *"six hundred sixty-six."* Yikes! *666, the Mark of the Devil.* (Maybe don't get this tattoo.)

Battle Stations

John turns toward Mount Zion and sees the Lamb and his 144,000 followers. Now they all have the Lamb's name and his Father's name barcoded on their foreheads. Harps are playing and the pure of heart are belting out songs. Angels whiz around uttering messages, "Fear God and give him glory, for the hour of his judgment has come. . . . If anyone worships the beast and its image, and receives a mark on his forehead or on his hand, he also shall drink the wine of God's wrath." Sounds like a bottle you don't want.

Jesus Christ sits on a white cloud with the golden crown and *sickle in his hand.* Angels with sickles start hacking wildly on earth, cutting everyone down. Blood flows "as high as a horse's bridle."

Seven Angels and Seven Plagues

A loud voice commands, "Go and pour out on the earth the *seven bowls of the wrath of God."* One bowl would've been quite enough, but here they come.

"So the first angel went and poured his bowl on the earth, and foul and evil sores came upon the men who bore the mark of the beast and worshiped its image."

"The second angel poured his bowl into the sea, and it became like the blood of a dead man, and every living thing died that was in the sea."

"The third angel poured his bowl into the rivers and the fountains of water, and they became blood."

"The fourth angel poured his bowl on the sun, and it was allowed to scorch men with fire; men were scorched by the fierce heat, and they *cursed the name of God* who had power over these plagues, and they did not repent and give him glory."

"The fifth angel poured his bowl on the throne of the beast, and its kingdom was in darkness; men gnawed their tongues in anguish." That has got to hurt.

"The sixth angel poured his bowl on the great river Euphrates, and its water was dried up, to prepare the way for the kings from the east. And I saw, issuing from the mouth of the dragon and from the mouth of the beast and from the mouth of the false prophet, three foul spirits like frogs, for they are demonic spirits, performing signs, who go abroad to the kings of the whole world, to assemble them for battle. . . . And they assembled them at the place which is called in Hebrew, *Armaged'don*."

"The seventh angel poured his bowl into the air, and a loud voice came out of the temple, from the throne, saying, '*It is done!*' And there were flashes of lightning, voices, peals of thunder, and a great earthquake such as had never been since men were on the earth, so great was that earthquake. The great city was split into three parts, and the cities of the nations fell, and God remembered great Babylon, to make her drain the cup of the fury of his wrath. And every island fled away, and no mountains were to be found; and great hailstones, heavy as a hundred weight, dropped on men from heaven."

Whore of Babylon

John is recording all the action when one of the seven angels comes over and says, "Come, I will show you the judgment of the *great harlot* who is seated upon many waters with whom the kings of the earth have committed fornication."

The angel transports John away into the wilderness where he sees "a woman sitting on a scarlet beast which was full of blasphemous names, and it had seven heads and ten horns. The woman was arrayed in purple and scarlet, and bedecked with gold and jewels and pearls, holding in her hand a golden cup full of abominations, and on her forehead was written a name of mystery: *'Babylon the great, mother of harlots and of the earth's abominations.'*"

Many readers think Babylon represents the Roman Empire. John unloads a rant of confusing references and put-downs of anyone associated with it, people like merchants, leaders, sailors, etc. "*Fallen, fallen is Babylon the great! It has become a dwelling place of demons. . . . In one hour judgment has come.*"

John rails on for quite some time in this bizarre political detour against Babylon. If Babylon is indeed Rome, it looks like ol' John is venting a torrent of rage at the Romans for exiling him to the rock island of Patmos. I guess if he just came out and called it Rome, his chances before the next parole board would be bleak.

Back to the End of the World

A full-scale barrage of Amens, Hallelujahs, Salvations, and Exultations spew forth. The heavens open, "Behold, a white horse! He who sat upon it is called Faithful and True, and in righteousness he judges and makes war. His eyes are like a flame of fire. He is clad in a robe dipped in blood, and the name by which he is called is the Word of God. And the armies of heaven, arrayed in fine linen, white and pure, followed him on white horses. From his mouth issues a sharp sword from which to smite the nations. . . . On his robe and on his thigh he has a name inscribed, *King of kings and Lord of lords*."

Another angel invites everyone to a "great supper of God," where they'll eat the flesh of those who fell, including their horses.

The sea beast and land beast are captured and thrown alive into "*the lake of fire that burns with sulphur. And the rest were slain by the sword of him who sits upon the horse, the sword that issues from his mouth; and all the birds were gorged with their flesh.*"

The dragon, "who is the Devil and Satan," is seized and chained in the bottomless pit, then the entrance is closed over for a thousand years. Strangely, "After that he must be loosed for a little while." Uh oh, smells like the makings of a spinoff sequel, or at least a million TV shows, books, movies, and action figures.

The martyrs, who had been beheaded for supporting Jesus and didn't wear the mark of the Devil, are reattached and now live with Jesus. The rest of the dead wait 1,000 years to be resurrected. This gives the martyrs some quality time alone with Christ before everyone else shows up.

After the thousand years, the dead rise and stand before God's white throne to be judged. The *Book of Life* is opened and "each is judged by what they have done" and any notes found in the book. The sea gives up her dead for judgment too. Death and Hades are thrown into the lake of fire. Oh, and for anyone whose name is not found in the Book of Life? Well, they're just tossed into the lake too. Seriously, zero tolerance.

Oops! Satan does get loose after 1,000 years and deceives nations into fighting for him, but they are all quickly sautéed by heavenly fire, and the Devil gets deposited into the same lake as the others.

John sees a new heaven and a new earth, followed by a new Jerusalem. God now lives with men and they are his people. Pain, crying, and mourning are things of the past. *"Behold, I make all things new."*

One of the seven bowls-of-wrath angels takes John on a tour of the new sparkling Jerusalem, complete with measurements and details. No temple is needed, because God dwells alongside men.

But (there's that omnipresent "but" again), "As for the cowardly, the faithless, the polluted, as for murderers, fornicators, sorcerers, idolaters, and all liars, their lot shall be in the lake that burns with fire and sulfur, which is the second death."

John certifies, just in case anyone is wondering, "These words are trustworthy and true."

The wild ride of the Book of Revelation and Holy Bible ends with these words: "He who testifies to these things says, 'Surely I am coming soon.' Amen. Come, Lord Jesus! The grace of the Lord Jesus be with all the saints. Amen."

Epilogue: Final Thoughts

So there you have it, a tour of the greatest bestseller of all time, the Holy Bible. About 1.500 pages of small print, of which 1,400 seem to be an unbelievable waste of papyrus.

After reading the volume cover to cover, it seems clear to me that these stories started out as an attempt by primitive man to explain what he knew of the natural world. A way to try to make sense of nature and try to steer it the way he wanted.

Over time and generations, stories that may have been fun around the campfire, somehow got elevated to the Word of God Himself. How did this happen? There's no evidence provided, and no basis to justify these beliefs within the text of the Bible.

Yet these stories have led to the creation of mega institutions with vast depositories of wealth, billions of followers, complex sets of rules and rituals, legions of employees, claims to territory, and direct influence on many governments and their policies.

What struck me most during this project was that the original source material for religious feasts, rituals, customs, and sacraments is surprisingly thin. A sentence or two, sandwiched between large passages of unnecessary prose, is plucked out and becomes a major doctrine of faith. Many passages themselves are inconsistent with other passages, and often contradictory. I found myself wondering repeatedly, "You mean that's all the support there is? Pretty flimsy."

It's mind-boggling to me that such a bloody and brutal book is still used, in the twenty-first century, to deny scientifically proven facts, condone discrimination, swear in our government leaders, and inform our policies.

But yet it is.

My guess is that most people who rely on its teachings haven't actually read the whole thing. And for those who have, they ignore vast sections and cherry-pick what they find useful. And for those who insist on its literal belief? Well, they have serious flaws in their mental functioning and judgment.

So, I hope you now have a perspective and background knowledge of what all the fuss is about!